Conversations with

BRANDO

Other books by Lawrence Grobel

The Hustons (1989)

Conversations with Capote (1985)

Conversations with

BRANDO

by Lawrence Grobel

HYPERION
NEW YORK

Library of Congress Cataloging-in-Publication Data

Grobel, Lawrence.
    Conversations with Brando/Lawrence Grobel.—1st ed.
      p. cm.
    ISBN 1-56282-990-4: $18.95
    1. Brando, Marlon—Interviews. 2. Actors—United States—
Interviews. I. Title.
PN2287.B683A3   1991
791.43′028′092—dc20   91–22998
                                     CIP

Design by Irva Mandelbaum

First Edition

10 9 8 7 6 5 4 3 2 1

For Hiromi

I should have been a pair of ragged claws
Scuttling across the floors of silent seas.

—T. S. Eliot
"The Love Song of J. Alfred Prufrock"

Contents

Photographs follow page 84.

INTRODUCTION

1 / "Listen, Do You Want to Do This in Tahiti?"

He only wants to talk about the *fucking* INDIANS!? Did you say to him that while he may not be an expert in history, he *is* one in ACTING?"

I could practically hear my editor's heart beating over the phone. I had finally broken through to Brando; after nearly a half year of negotiations he had actually picked up the phone and talked to me. As soon as we hung up I called my editor in New York to tell him the interview was on. Brando was willing to talk. Only he had certain restrictions. Like he only wanted to talk about . . . Indians.

Brando's focus didn't bother me nearly as much as it did Barry Golson, my editor at *Playboy*. Because I knew that if we could just get started, other topics of conversation would be covered. I was prepared to talk to him about Indians for as long as it took him to talk himself out. That was my strategy. To read as many books and prepare as many questions on the American Indian as I could. If it took hours of talk and days of meetings to warm up Marlon

Brando, I figured it would be worth it, as the man hadn't given any in-depth interviews since Truman Capote went to Japan during the making of *Sayonara* in 1956 and pinned him so neatly for a *New Yorker* profile.

Besides, I had, during the six months of dealing with his secretary, Alice Marchak, developed a relationship over the phone with the woman who was closest to him, who knew him as well as anyone. And she told me, "Once he starts talking, without even realizing it, he holds nothing back, he just talks." I was counting on that more than on Marlon's preliminary restrictions to bookend Capote's twenty-two-year-old interview with the country's preeminent actor.

"I've read so many interviews of people who are not qualified to give answers to questions asked," Brando said when we first talked on the phone. "Just because people are famous and well known, questions are often asked them and they're unqualified to answer: questions on economics; neuter archaeological discoveries in Tuscany; what do they think of the recent virulent form of gonorrhea? And I used to answer those questions and then I'd ask myself what the fuck am I doing? It's absolutely preposterous I should be asked those questions and equally preposterous I found myself answering."

Brando wasn't angry when he said this, instead, he started to laugh. He appreciated the absurdity. "I don't know a fucking thing about economics, mathematics, or anything else," he said.

Which was fine by me, since I had no intention of asking him about things he didn't know anything about. But he *did* know more about the way the world worked than most of us. He certainly knew about fame, celebrity, the FBI, the problems facing the black and red man, illusion and reality, harboring fugitives, owning and operating a thirteen-island atoll in the South Pacific, disguises, pretenses, high finance, exploitation. That was why, when his secretary said he wanted to see my questions, I sent instead a list of broad topics, meant more to make him smile than to be taken seriously. Among the topics were: Social Causes, the Environment, Politics, Religion, Acting, Women, the Arts, the World!

"Was it you who sent me a copy of stuff you wanted to talk about?" he asked me.

"Those were just topics," I said. "I was just trying to cover everything."

"Yeah, but rather than running into the situation of saying, 'I don't think I can usefully comment on that,' fourteen times, I think we should come to some understanding before it happens. Those topics had to do with my personal life and a lot of other things and had nothing to do with Indians and I assumed that the interview was going to be about Indians."

"I've always assumed that as well," I said. At least until he ran out of things to say about them.

"It would be difficult for you, Larry, to ask the right questions about Indians and this might sound ridiculous and against your journalistic impulse but if I can supply you with some of the critical information, then you could ask me the questions. I mean everyone, almost all of us, is completely ignorant about Indians: who they are, what their relationship to the United States is, what they feel about being the invisible people of this country. People often ask questions about basket-weaving and that's totally irrelevant. Now I in no way mean to be a spokesman for Indians, but I have a wide spectrum of representation and I do want their voices and opinions heard."

I had no problem with Brando supplying me with critical information, though I suspected he never would. I just wanted to pin down an actual date for us to begin. It was January 23, 1978, when we had this initial conversation and Brando suggested we begin on February 1. It would actually take another five and a half months before I met him, but at least progress had been made.

During those months I studied enough about the man to know that he was considered by many to be the world's greatest living actor, the man who changed the style of the movies, the most influential and widely imitated actor of his generation. He burst onto our consciousness wearing a torn T-shirt, mumbling, growling, scowling, screaming for "Stel-la!" as Stanley Kowalski in Tennessee Williams's *A Streetcar Named Desire,* first on Broadway, then on film. It marked the beginning of a career that was to be as wild as many of the characters he so expertly portrayed.

An intensely private man, Brando stirs emotions and elicits reactions that go beyond his status as either actor or political activist. He's been called brilliant, a lout, considerate, arrogant, gentle, selfish. He has passed into myth, become history. Among the highest paid and most respected actors in America, he is one of the artists who will doubtless be remembered well into the next century.

From the beginning, Brando unleashed a raw power that had never been seen before on the screen. He talked through his body, affecting viewers emotionally each time he got beat up and stood up. What audiences knew of courage they saw enacted by Brando time and time again, from *The Men* to *On the Waterfront* to *Viva Zapata!* And what they thought was evil was reinterpreted and given new dimensions as Brando became a wild punk hoodlum, a Nazi officer, a kidnapper, a bandit, an Ugly American Ambassador, a Mafia chief.

Like a figure in a classical Greek drama, after rising to the top during the fifties, his career plummeted to disappointing lows in the sixties. Yet, when people thought he had nothing left to give, he mounted a magnificent and stunning comeback with *The Godfather* and *Last Tango in Paris,* a film so brutally and sexually honest that it was hailed as adding a new dimension to the art.

Born in Omaha, Nebraska, on April 3, 1924, "Bud," as he was called, had lived in three states and five locations by the time he was six years old. His father, whom Brando described as "a strong, wild man who liked to fight and drink," was a manufacturer of chemical feed products and insecticides. His mother, who also had a drinking problem, was a semiprofessional actress, who once appeared with Henry Fonda in a 1928 production of a Eugene O'Neill play.

An athlete but a poor student, Brando was expelled from Libertyville High School for smoking during his junior year. His mother wanted to send him to an experimental school for problem students, but his father's will prevailed and he was sent to Shattuck Military Academy in Faribault, Minnesota, in 1942. Unable to take "the military asylum" seriously, he was expelled when one of his many pranks literally backfired: he had placed a "bomb" of firecrackers against a teacher's bedroom door, ran a line of hair tonic from it to his own door, lit it, and watched the evidence burn into the wooden floor.

Returning home, he told his parents he would enter the ministry. They talked him out of it. Then he thought he'd become a musician, as he had a passion for playing the bongo drums. When no one hired his five-piece band, he worked for six weeks laying irrigation ditches for a construction company. Eventually, he drifted to New York, following his two older sisters who had studied acting and painting. It was 1943 and he enrolled in Erwin Piscator's Dramatic Workshop at the New School for Social Research. His teacher was Stella Adler, a disciple of Konstantin Stanislavsky, who believed in discovering a role from the inside out.

Under Adler's tutelage, Brando took acting seriously. He demonstrated a love for makeup, wigs, and foreign accents, and he began studying philosophy, French, dance, fencing, and yoga. What he did mostly, however, was observe others' characteristics and translate them into revealing gestures.

He dressed in jeans and T-shirts, lived in numerous cheap apartments and, like most beginning actors, stood in unemployment lines. Occasionally, he worked at odd jobs, such as being a night watchman or an elevator boy at Best's department store. For a while, he roomed with an old school friend, Wally Cox, who eventually moved out because he could no longer tolerate Brando's pet raccoon.

He debuted in New York as Jesus Christ in a 1944 Dramatic Workshop production of Gerhart Hauptmann's *Hannele's Way to Heaven*. He followed that with small parts in plays by Molière and Shakespeare. That summer the Dramatic Workshop students performed in Sayville, Long

Island, where casting agent Maynard Morris "discovered" Brando. Morris got him some screen tests and then recommended he audition for the Rodgers and Hammerstein production of *I Remember Mama* by John Van Druten. With Stella Adler encouraging him, Brando auditioned, got the part, and spent the next year earning $75 a week playing the oldest son of immigrant Norwegians.

During this time, another older woman entered his life: agent Edith Van Cleve, who recognized the young actor's raw energy. She got him other auditions, none of them clicking until Stella Adler convinced her husband, producer-director Harold Clurman, to cast Brando in Maxwell Anderson's *Truckline Cafe*. Determined to make him stop mumbling and articulate, Clurman had Brando climbing ropes, screaming, falling, being kicked around the stage during rehearsals. The effort worked, but the play didn't, closing within two weeks. Brando, though, was noticed. A young Pauline Kael remembers feeling embarrassed for him—"I looked up and saw what I thought was an actor having a seizure onstage"—until she realized he was *acting*.

In 1946 he appeared in George Bernard Shaw's *Candida*, and also toured outside New York in *Antigone*. In the fall he appeared with Paul Muni in *A Flag Is Born*, about the plight of stateless Jews. It was his first involvement in a political cause and the money raised was sent to the League for a Free Palestine. A year later, when Williams completed *A Streetcar Named Desire*, Brando was ready to make himself known.

There are those who saw him as the ruthless, savage, sexy Kowalski during his year-and-a-half-long run on Broadway who can still describe the way he moved onstage. Critics quickly hailed him as the most gifted actor of his generation. But the role was demanding and led Brando into analysis, which lasted for a decade. It also led him into films, which he openly disdained but which offered him the opportunity to make more money, work fewer hours, and reach a wider audience. Brando went to Hollywood and never returned to Broadway.

From 1950 to 1955, Brando starred in eight films, the first six of which, as actor Jon Voight said, "were absolutely enormous." Those films were *The Men, A Streetcar Named Desire, Viva Zapata!, Julius Caesar, The Wild One,* and *On the Waterfront.* Brando had established the Method as the acting force to contend with.

The director who had the most influence on him was Elia Kazan, who directed him in *Streetcar, Zapata!,* and *Waterfront.* Kazan called him "the only genius I ever met in the field of acting." Kim Hunter, who played his wife, Stella, in *Streetcar,* spoke of his "uncanny sense of the truth. Anything you do that may not be true shows up immediately as false with him." Bette Davis said, "He has always transcended the techniques he was taught. His consequent glamor and style have nothing to do with self-involvement but rather radiation." Sir John Gielgud, who worked with him in *Julius Caesar,* called him a "thrilling artist." Paul Muni spoke of his "magnificent, great gift."

That great gift was recognized in 1955 when he won the Oscar for Best Actor for his role as Terry Malloy in *On the Waterfront,* which he accepted. Eighteen years later, he won his second Oscar, for his role as Don Vito Corleone in *The Godfather,* but by then, Brando's social consciousness had risen dramatically and he disdained awards, refusing to accept it and asking an American Indian woman to stand before the academy and the world to explain why.

Between *On the Waterfront* and *The Godfather,* Brando made nineteen pictures (he's made thirty-three in his thirty-nine-year career to date, including *Superman, Apocalypse Now, The Formula, A Dry White Season,* and *The Freshman*). Some of them have been strong and sensitive, such as the *Young Lions, Reflections in a Golden Eye, Burn!,* and *The Nightcomers;* and some have been embarrassing and trite, such as *A Countess from Hong Kong* (written and directed by Charles Chaplin) and *Candy*. But whatever the role, his acting has consistently surprised and often confused his audience with its unpredictability.

Often cited as a spoiled, temperamental, stubborn star, Brando was blamed for the financial failures of pictures like *Mutiny on the Bounty,* which went $12 million over budget, *Burn!,* when he insisted the production move from South America to Africa, and *One-Eyed Jacks,* which he directed over a three-year period before Paramount finally took it away from him.

Throughout his career, Brando has preferred to speak out on issues of social importance rather than on acting and the movies, involving himself in causes far removed from make-believe. He has actively participated in marches and spoken out on behalf of the Jews, the blacks, the American Indians, the downtrodden and the poor, and against capital punishment, bigotry, awards, most politicians, and policing organizations whenever they seem to infringe upon individual rights and freedoms. For UNESCO, he flew to India during a famine; in the state of Washington, he was arrested for participating in an Indian fish-in over river rights; in Gresham, Wisconsin, he ducked bullets along with radical Indians from the Menominee tribe demanding a return of disputed land. Attacking critics who dubbed him insincere, Shana Alexander wrote in a *Newsweek* column, "No American I can think of has taken his own initiative to reduce injustice in this world more often, and been knocked down for it more often, than Marlon Brando."

His relationships with mostly foreign women have been mysterious and often stormy. He has been legally married and divorced twice: in 1957, to British actress Anna Kashfi, who had claimed to be of East Indian origin, and in 1960, to Mexican actress Movita. He had a child with each woman and, for a dozen years, he publicly battled through the courts with his first wife for custody of their son, Christian. In Tahiti for *Mutiny on the Bounty* in 1960, he met his costar, Tarita, with whom he has two children, Teihotu and Cheyenne.

While in Tahiti, he discovered Tetiaroa, an atoll forty miles north of Papeete. When it came up for sale, he purchased it. Ever since, he's divided his time between his home on Mulholland Drive in Beverly Hills and living like Robinson Crusoe on his islands in Tahiti.

"Listen, do you want to do this in Tahiti?" Brando asked me over the phone on March 28, 1978. He was very abrupt and businesslike. He thought the middle of April would be good, although he had a deposition in court to deal with and couldn't be sure if it could be postponed or thrown out. Once I agreed, he thought there might be a story about Tahiti as well as the Indians, but he didn't want to entwine the two.

"Tahiti does not have income, except through tourism,

so maybe we could do a separate story. They have no raw materials, so the only way I can help the economy now is to give some interest to tourism. But I can't give short shrift or a kind of ricochet version of what's happening with the American Indians. I'm not really interested in talking about acting, the theater, my personal life—I never talk about that, it's odious to me. It's meaningless really. It's gossip trade."

I kept quiet. I didn't want to agree not to talk to him about anything.

"To some extent we could talk about the environment," he added, "and as part of one of the problems that faces any environment is the social environment, and that is certainly cheek by jowl with the Indian issue. So maybe those two things could dovetail."

When I said I saw no problem with that he then apologized for delaying this interview for so long. "I want to say that I'm disturbed by the fact you've been getting this extended round-around from me. It's just been one crazy thing after another." (Here he interrupted himself to shout at Alice Marchak, whose voice I heard in the background, "I'm not blaming you for Christ's sake!")

As soon as I hung up with him, Alice Marchak called. "I got you a trip to Tahiti," she said with some satisfaction. It was she who suggested we do it there after Marlon started having doubts when we could possibly talk since he wanted to go to Tahiti as soon as he completed his business in Los Angeles. "It's good you're going," she said, "you'll see a more personal Marlon." Then she stuttered a bit trying to gently phrase the self-censorship Marlon expected me to apply. "Without him telling you he'll expect you to

13

know what is private and what is not," she finally said.

When I asked her what to expect on the island, she answered, "Not much. There isn't much to do at night. Marlon stays up late talking on his ham radio." She then ran down a list of things I should bring: Lomatil for the inevitable diarrhea, Band-Aids, a flashlight to walk from one bungalow to another, a plastic raincoat, an anti-itch cream, Cutter's ointment, sandals, sneakers, bathing suit, snorkel, silicone packets to absorb moisture and protect my tape recorder and batteries, tetanus and gamma globulin shots.

I wondered what I might bring Marlon as a peace offering before we began our talks. She suggested that William Colby's new book on the CIA would interest him. I remembered how Capote brought a bottle of vodka when he saw Brando and got him to loosen up that way. Alice confirmed that he liked a good Russian vodka or a good tequila, but said he really wasn't much of a drinker. "One drink and he's flying," she said, laughing at stories she often heard of Brando's excessive drinking on airplanes. "Marlon doesn't like to fly, he's afraid of flying," Alice said. "So if a pretty stewardess asks him if he wants a drink, he'll say yeah, and keep saying yeah as long as she asks."

Alice liked to talk on the phone and with only gentle prodding she would tell me what it was like working for Brando for twenty-two years. "He does not make decisions," she said. "I'll ask him coffee or tea? It's a half hour for him to decide, then he'll say, 'Make me whatever, I just want something to drink.' He forces me to make decisions. You cannot pin him down. On anything. Anything. I don't care what it is. He can say what he doesn't want, but he can't say what he wants. If I say, 'Are you going to go today or tomorrow?' He'll say, 'Don't talk to me now.' He'll say to me, 'I really would like a sweater.' I'll say, 'What kind do you want?' 'A sweater, Alice! How many kinds are there?' 'There's turtlenecks, cardigans . . .' 'Well, you know, the kind I wear.' So I'll buy him a black turtleneck sweater and he'll put it on and say, 'I didn't want a turtle-neck.' It's that kind of thing. 'I didn't want black, I wanted wine color. You can never be wrong, why don't you admit you were wrong, you got me the wrong sweater.' He can't stand when I'm right. Marlon cannot stand losing and he cannot stand a woman besting him. The other day he said to me, 'Alice, are you trying to tell me how to die?' He was standing in the kitchen running lukewarm tap water into a cup for twenty minutes waiting for it to get hot. I said, 'Marlon, that's not the way. All you have to do is put the cup of water in the microwave and in one minute it will be hot.' He just looked at me and then, of course, he went and got his watch to time it. I was right, it took one minute. He hates it when I'm right. But his idiosyncrasies don't bother me, they just amuse me. The only thing he's consistent about is his inconsistencies.

"Trying to get him to even pick up the telephone is some-thing. He said something very interesting one day. 'You know Alice, you'd be shocked at the reputation you have. People think you are the toughest girl in the world. They think you keep everybody away from me, you've isolated me, they can't reach me by phone, can't come up here.' I said, 'You've got to be joking.' He said, 'I'm not, it's true. People say they've been trying to reach me for days and I say, 'Oh, Alice never told me.' All through the years he's blamed me for everything that he never wanted to do. I not only give him all of his calls, but I type them out."

In May, Marlon's other secretary, Caroline, called to say that Marlon wanted me to write him a letter outlining specific areas I wanted to discuss and then he would have a lawyer draw up an agreement for me to sign. I took a deep breath and said no. Either he trusted me or he didn't.

Fearing the interview was in jeopardy, I decided instead to send Brando a mailgram indicating that I saw what we were about to embark on as a general, free-ranging interview and not a narrow one-topic discussion bound by legal parameters. The next day Caroline called and said there'd be nothing to sign, I should plan to come in June.

2 / Ten Days on Brando's Island

June 13: Day One

I'm sitting next to Marlon's Tahitian wife, Tarita, in the small twin engine plane that's taking us to Brando's island. We're flying into thick gray clouds, and Tarita is frightened. She thinks we should turn back. Dick Johnson, Marlon's accountant, reassures her. "I called the island," he says, "it's not raining there."

Suddenly the sun is gone and rain pelts the plane's windows. Tarita clutches her seven-year old daughter, Cheyenne. The pilot flies through the storm. Below us is Tetiaroa: thirteen small flat islets, each covered with palm trees, arranged around a turquoise lagoon. We land on the airstrip of the only island that's inhabited. The plane taxis the width of the island and stops a few yards from Marlon's bungalow.

Brando is waiting. He kisses Tarita on both cheeks, then comes to greet me. He is wearing an Indian cotton hooded shirt and pants, and with his gray-white hair, paunch, and wry, warm smile he has the appearance of an East Indian holy man. He jokes about his outfit, which he says he designed because he is prone to sunstroke and must keep covered. He takes my bag and leads me to a thatched roof bungalow. Everything but the cement floor in the octagonal room is made from palm trees. Brando comments on my sandals which, he says, will not last because sand will get between my toes and the leather.

"You can tell a man's education by the spread of his toes," he says, making one of the seemingly random remarks that pepper his conversation. He puts his own bare feet on the windowsill. "If the toes are widespread, they grew up shoeless," he says, and then he proceeds to launch into a discourse on the nature of Tahitians. For two hours, he talks—of primitive tribes "looking through two thousand years of history with ballpoint pens through their noses," of the Untouchables in India, American blacks, Haitians, Africans, Japanese, Pakistanis, Polynesians.

He talks about his ambitions for his island. He'd like to build a school for the blind here and invite oceanographers to come and conduct experiments. He's had forty scientists and a Japanese archaeologist check the land and he's had aerial photographs taken. But he's had to curtail the various projects because things tend to fall apart when he's gone. "You can't bring culture here, you have to adapt to theirs," he says, swiping at some annoying flies, catching two in his hand. And Tahitians, he says, do not have goals or ambitions. "Nothing bothers them, if they have flies, they live with them. The flies breed in the fallen coconuts, and unless you go around picking up all the coconuts you can't get rid of them. But tell a Tahitian that and he doesn't believe it."

He is impressed with the Tahitians' ability to read body language. "They can appear as if they aren't paying attention but they can remember if you wore socks or not, if your pants were clean, the color of your shoes."

Most people who come down, he says, get bored after a few weeks. You have to find yourself, your inner resources. "When I first get here I'm like a discharged battery. It takes a few weeks to unwind, but eventually the island's slower rhythms sink in." He has stayed up to six months at one time. His shortest stay was three days. "When people come here to see me, they're usually all wound up, they talk fast, they've got projects, ideas, deals. And I sit here like a whale."

A cool wind blows through the windows. The bungalow is close to the water's edge. Directly across the lagoon is another island. There are pigs on that one, he says. He'd like to bring over some wild animals—elephants, gorillas. But he's concerned they'd be neglected when he's gone. "Must bring up animals like a child."

I ask him about his children's education. He prefers to keep Teihotu and Cheyenne in Tahiti, where they can learn to enjoy life and nature. He doesn't approve of the peer pressure in America. "Teenagers are the most conformist of people. They are anything but radical. You've got to learn the right words, dress the right way."

He asks if I'm hungry and we take a walk to his bungalow. He points out the plants growing in the sand in front of his door, which he says he waters with his urine. I notice the tall antenna in front of his hut, which he had built "out of rage because the phones are so bad." Inside, there are two double beds, shelves of books and cassettes, a bottle of Rolaids, packages of grape Double Bubble sugarless gum. Researching *Apocalypse Now* he read a stack of books which all told the same story: how our being there was all for gain, what Vietnam had was rubber, oil, raw materials. "All the bullshit and propaganda about freedom—hogwash."

He shows me his ham radio, which must constantly be "cooked" to keep away the mildew. He sits down and twirls the dial. Foreign music and languages come over the radio. "That's China, their anthem . . . that's Mexico . . . that's Cuba."

The flies continue to bother him. He slaps at one that lands on him, swipes at others that fly by. His hands are as fast as a lizard's tongue. "If you could take all the time you spend poised to catch flies and put it together you'd have a pretty neat vacation," he observes. Brando says he was once influenced by the Jain philosophy, which holds that one shouldn't kill anything, not even a fly. He says it made sense for a while, until he thought it through—and realized how, with every breath you take, you're killing something.

His accountant, Dick, the island foreman, William, and Tarita come by to discuss island business. I get up and Marlon tells me to feel free to explore the island. "I'll come by later," he says. "We can watch the sun set. There's sometimes a touch of green just as it drops."

Along the beach I watch hand-sized crabs crawling along the sand in their shells. Palm sprouts grow out of fallen coconuts. Palm trees curved according to how the wind was blowing when they were growing. An abundance of coral, shells, black sea cucumbers, at the bottom of the clear water. Gentle lapping of the water on the shore. Lush clouds, blue sky, discarded radio batteries.

The wind begins to blow. Rain comes and goes. In my toilet, a large cockroach floats.

Dinner. Marlon comes to get me. We are joined by Dick, Brando's secretary, Caroline, and her six-year-old daughter. The dining room has twenty tables, nineteen of them empty. We eat meat, potatoes, fish, salad, ice cream, fruit, and cheese. Marlon says he's on a diet so he doesn't eat the bread. He asks me if I ever saw *Mondo Cane*. Tells a story of a woman in Hong Kong who brought her toy poodle to a restaurant and the waiter took it, cooked it, and fed it to her. We laugh. Marlon is entertaining, expressive. Laments that he can't remember things. Picks up a place mat and says there are ways to remember, if you had connecting stories for each line in the place mat.

After dinner, Marlon and I walk out on the short, narrow pier. He says he'd like to build a lifting hydraulic patio on the pier that would work on the principle of the wind. It could raise you twenty feet and lower you when the wind died down. Explains how transmitters work, how humpback whales can be heard singing for five hundred miles. He's full of random bits of arcane knowledge.

Walking back he picks off a small white flower from a tree and says, "Smell this. You can sometimes smell the island before you see it because of these."

From a bungalow, I hear the sound of television. Tarita and other Tahitians are watching. Marlon prefers silence, but he's made the concession. TV brought the Twist to Tahiti in twenty minutes, he says.

June 14: Day Two

Brando is tied up with island business: developing tourism, building a house on the other side of the island, supervising new construction of a reception area, having roofs re-thatched. He's in conflict over tourists coming to his island. He's tired of having them snap pictures of him and at one point closed down the hotel and fired thirty-five people. But for tax purposes, and because it's expensive to keep pouring money into the island, he has reopened it for one- and two-day tours. Because there is a limited amount of water, tourism can never fully develop. "He'll always be losing money," Dick tells me.

I walk around the island, snorkel, and swim on the other side which opens into a magnificent bay.

In the evening Marlon and I take a walk, stretch out on the sand, and talk for three hours. He is eloquent, passionate, outrageous. "That star next to the moon is always there," he says, looking up at the night sky. "I remember I was in Marrakech on a sparkling, crystalline desert night and I saw the same star. I'd been talking to this girl a long time— it was four in the morning—and the muezzin came out on his minaret and started chanting. It was an enchanted moment. It made me feel like I was in Baghdad in the twelfth century." I ask him if the girl he was with was a Moslem. "Nah," he says, "airline hostess."

He then changes the subject to American Indians. Says some Indians hate him because he's white. He talks of hustling, and how he's never promoted himself or his movies. Even a writer like Saul Bellow, he complains, goes on TV to hustle his work just like everybody else. Brando also speaks of poets he likes, Dylan Thomas and Kenneth Patchen, and quotes one of Patchen's small poems:

> Wait   wait
>   wait   wait
>   now.

I bring up T. S. Eliot's "The Love Song of J. Alfred Prufrock" and he says, "If the mermaids can't sing for me here, Christ, they never will."

June 15: Day Three

"My favorite interview," Marlon is saying, "was on television with Mrs. Arnold Palmer. The interviewer asked, 'Is there any special ritual that you go through before your husband plays?' She says, 'No.' 'Nothing at all?' 'Well, I kiss his balls.' The interviewer did a double take. 'You mean his golf balls, right?' 'Of course,' Mrs. Palmer said, 'what did you think I meant?' "

I was hoping this was a prelude to our sitting down with the tape recorder on, but Marlon's got another day of island meetings before we can begin. "I'm not business-oriented," he says. "I could have been a multimillionaire but then I would have had to have been that kind of a person, and I'm not." He adds that if *Superman* is as big a hit as they say it's going to be he'll make a lot of money because he's got a percentage. (According to Dick Johnson, when Marlon finished shooting *Superman,* for which he was paid between $2 and $3 million, he returned to Tetiaroa and said to Dick, "Twelve days work, cash on the line, who's worth that kind of money?" "Nobody I know," Dick answered.)

Before dinner I join Marlon at the bar. His meetings are over, Dick has flown back to Papeete. The bartender is a German named George who has floated around Tahiti for twenty years working at different hotels. He has come to Tetiaroa to serve the workers in the evenings and any guests who might visit the island. Marlon asks him questions, studies him. William comes by. He says he's been saving a very powerful palm wine drink for Marlon to taste. It's been fermenting six months. Brando says to bring it and we both have a glass. He tells me he's had some really wild parties on the island. "Once, we got six kinds of drunk, it went all night. Tahitians can drink, party, fuck, sleep, drink, party, fuck, all through the night. I can't do that. Once I'm drunk I'm out."

Apropos of nothing Marlon states, "Next to the gonads, the most important organs we have are our eyes. How ridiculous to put them right near where the fighting instrument is." He means the mouth. Where would he put the eyes? "The neck," he says. "But isn't that where an animal would go, for the neck?" I ask. "Well, you need three places," he mutters, but it occurs to him you need binary vision, thus two eyes must be in each place. It gets too complicated to figure out where one's eyes would be safest.

The one drink is enough for Marlon. He talks of psychics, mediums, and clairvoyants. They're mostly fakes, he says, but he believes in Peter Hurkos, who once came close to guessing what object Brando had carefully concealed inside a lucite box which he had wrapped in twine. It was an old nail from the original "Bounty" that a bald-headed man had given to him. Hurkos said that the object was weathered and had been given to Brando by a balding man. "I could have put anything into that box," Marlon says, "a pig's knuckle, a fingernail." He's also interested in the parapsychological work of a former high school classmate of his, Dr. Thelma Moss of UCLA.

He asks William how to say red and yellow in Tahitian. Each word is pronounced twice. Marlon has always had a talent for languages.

After dinner we take a walk. There's a circle of light around the half moon. White birds dive into the water. The sky sparkles with stars and falling meteorites. I ask Marlon if a UFO landed in front of him would he go? Most celebrities I've asked that question—like Barbra Streisand or Dolly Parton—have said definitely not, they wouldn't take the risk of entering the unknown and *being* unknown. But Marlon says, "Of course." He doesn't believe that such things actually happen. "The odds that both we would be exploring space and space would be exploring us within a span of a thousand years would be incredible." That we've only been exploring for twenty-five years and there have been so many sightings makes him believe that our government is far more advanced than we know, and all those peculiar movements in the sky are secret experiments which the government has refused to reveal.

He picks up a handful of sand. "There are probably more individual grains in two handfuls of sand than there are stars in the universe," he says.

I've brought my tape recorder with me and turn it on. We talk for a while but I am distracted by what appears to be a white blur crossing over the lagoon. The second time it occurs I interrupt Marlon who jumps up like a shot anxious to see what I've seen. "Christ, why didn't you tell me? I can always talk." Once he and Tarita were lying on the sand and she saw something blue rise out of the sea and come down again. She grabbed him tightly, digging her nails into his arm in fear. "I'm always looking for that sort of stuff," he says.

June 16: Day Four

We tape all afternoon, six hours. Brando's a bit pontifical at times but that's to be expected. Beginning sessions are usually strategy sessions. He must have caught two dozen flies.

He gives me two things to read: the *Government Misconduct Associated with the Dennis Banks/Russell Means Wounded Knee Trial*, and the transcript of the trial proceedings of *United States* v. *Russell Means and Dennis Banks*.

At dinner he is quiet. He counts the newly inlaid wooden strips in the ceiling and wonders how long it will last. He breaks the silence with a question: "So what do you think's going to happen in Kananga?" Rhodesia might straighten itself out, he says, but South Africa is going to explode.

Afterwards, out on the pier, he watches the lagoon. "If you had a thirty-four-foot aluminum straw and you were going to suck up Fanta, you could only get it thirty-three feet because that's all a vacuum pump can pump," he says.

Then he gets on his belly and stares at the water. He's puzzled by changes in the current. He says he's never seen anything like it in the fifteen years he's been visiting his island. He seems very concerned.

June 17: Day Five

"Another day in paradise," Marlon says with a laugh at breakfast. He entertains Caroline's daughter by closing his eyes and swiping at a group of flies buzzing around the grapefruit. He asks her to guess how many he's caught. She says three. He flings them onto the floor and they count. Eight. While she is counting he catches another fly and pops it into his mouth. When she looks at him he opens his mouth and the fly comes out.

He spends the morning talking on his ham radio, using another name and never revealing his true identity. He talks with someone living underground conducting medical experiments at the South Pole. A man living five hundred miles west of Miami tells him how lightning once went through his phone and burned his wife's nose. A third connection is a man who is into contests. "I'm not really interested in talking about contests," Marlon says. One transmission clears up a mystery. Brando finds out that there was an earthquake in Samoa last night—the changing current he observed on the pier was the effect of a tidal wave caused by the quake.

He leaves the radio, listens for a moment, says a plane is coming. I hear nothing for a minute, then the faint sound of an engine. Marlon tells me he has very sensitive hearing. He's been to doctors about it because even the hitting of a spoon on a cup can irritate him. The doctors told him there was nothing wrong. "You hear what you want to hear," they said. "Maybe that's so," Marlon says now, "maybe it is psychological. Because sometimes I can't hear what people are saying. I can hear high-pitched noises and sounds, but I can't hear human voices."

The plane lands, bringing his seventeen-year-old son Teihotu and some friends. Tomorrow is Father's Day and they have come from Papeete, where they are still in school, to spend a few days. Marlon and Tarita greet them, then he returns to his bungalow as Tarita sweeps the compound. "I never saw anybody work as hard as Tarita," he says. "All she does is work."

We spend part of the day sitting on the sand looking out at the lagoon and the large coral rocks that form a line to break up any tall waves before they reach his bungalow. He spots a shell embedded in the rocks, gets a hammer and file, and starts banging out chunks of the coral to get at the shell. Then his daughter Cheyenne comes, bringing him some shells she has found. She is a beautiful, but moody, girl who speaks both English and French. Brando takes her shells and thanks her. When she runs off he says he saves everything she brings him.

I ask him if twenty years ago he could have lived the way he does now. He says no. "Once I was the only person here, absolutely alone on this island. I really like being alone," he says.

He goes inside, finds a strength-tester that measures the pressure it takes to make a light turn on, and says, "Here, you'll like this." He said Teihotu can do eighty-five pounds with both hands. I try. The light doesn't go on.

Towards evening I walk over to the bar and talk with George. I ask him if he knows who Marlon is. "An actor," George says. Is he aware that Brando's considered to be one of the world's greatest actors? "Auf, well, everybody's the greatest," George answers. "What I do, what he does, it's a business. He's an actor, I'm a bartender. People like me at what I do. I could be an actor."

June 18: Day Six

Although Marlon's feeling under the weather we are going on a picnic to another island. On the catamaran he asks, "How fast do you think we're going?" We all guess. "Twenty-two miles per hour," he answers, explaining that the catamaran goes twelve mph and the wind is adding another ten. He knows this because there are still flies on the boat and "flies can fly up to twenty-two miles per hour."

He gets out his Leicaflex and takes pictures of everyone. Focusing on Caroline, he says, "You've got snot in your nose." She almost falls for it.

A Tahitian who had trailed a line behind the catamaran hauls in a large fish. Then he removes the hook and chops the head. Brando is squeamish. "Isn't that horrible? But that's the nature of the beast. They don't want to eat corn-flakes."

When we reach the other island Marlon asks Teihotu to carry him on his back, he doesn't want to get wet. Teihotu complies.

We gather wood and start a fire to keep the flies and mosquitoes away. Tarita and her crew go off to fish by the reef. Marlon watches them from his blanket. He picks up a crab, plays with it, wedging a sliver of wood between the crab and its shell so he can examine it.

"Do you think you could make the Brooklyn Bridge out of all the bottle caps in the world?" he asks. When I say yes, he says, "Boy, you're sure of that one, aren't you?"

Someone wants a Sprite, someone else a Fanta, but there is no bottle opener. Marlon uses a Coke bottle to open the Fanta by pushing one cap under the other. But the wrong bottle opens and the Coke explodes all over his face and clothing. "Anybody want Coke?" he deadpans.

Tarita and the others return with dozens of spear-gunned multicolored fish. After eating and drinking, they start packing things. Marlon sits. "Nobody ever says, 'Let's go,'" he says. "Everyone just knows when it's time to leave." Cheyenne brings him his Father's Day present: a drawing she's done of the sea.

At dinner, a Tahitian woman is softly crying, waiting for Marlon to finish eating. Marlon sees her and gets up. She has come to complain of her boyfriend "husband" who had beat her up. He had been drinking and when he entered the kitchen she told him to do the dishes. He refused and belted her. Marlon goes to tell the man if he does it again he must leave the island. "Why they come to me, I don't know," he says when he returns. "It's my bat and ball, I guess."

June 19: Day Seven

"I find him an extraordinary man," Caroline says at breakfast while Marlon sleeps late. "He has the most incredible memory for details which often seem unimportant to us—the way your nails were cut, how you sat, what you wore, the way your hand fell upon your cheek." She says that he remembers all of Cole Porter's and Harold Arlen's song lyrics. She says he's not hassled as much in Los Angeles as he is in New York, where people are always taking his picture. When he travels he always leaves behind his luggage, cameras, whizzing through the airport, leaving his secretary to handle customs. He hates waiting around.

Caroline, whose mother is Japanese and father English, has never seen *Streetcar* or *On the Waterfront*.

Marlon comes by in the afternoon, a glob of sun cream on his nose. It's hot, there's no wind, and he calls to William to knock out three more windows in my bungalow so the air can circulate better. He picks up my telescope, looks through it, and says, "This is a ten-power." I ask him how he knew and he talks about looking through it with one eye and opening the other eye and measuring the distance between both views. What he actually did was read on the telescope that it was ten-power.

As we walk back to his bungalow he says, "I bet Caroline you wouldn't say anything about this shit on my nose." "You won," I say.

31

He notices a large hole in a tree's branch. "That's where mosquitoes breed," he says, getting a shovel and filling the hole with sand, dirt, and a plant which he uproots.

That evening, another bet. Marlon says the dinner gong was beaten, Caroline says it wasn't. The loser has to stand on a table and sing and dance. They ask me if the signal had been given and I say yes. Marlon looks pleased and insists Caroline pay the bet. Embarrassed, she climbs onto a table and does a two-step while singing "Somewhere Over the Rainbow." After a few bars she gets down, but Marlon says, "No, you have to finish." She gets back onto the table. There is a cruel satisfaction in Marlon's eyes.

I ask him if he loses many bets. "No, I don't," he answers. "I've been very lucky."

When Caroline drinks a Coke, Marlon says she shouldn't because it's too fattening. "It is not," she says, "there are only eighty calories in a six-ounce glass." Marlon sees doubt in her eyes and jumps on her, claiming there are at least two hundred calories. He wants to bet. She's game. He comes up with this: the loser has to sell used tires on the corner of Mulholland and Laurel Canyon in L.A. during rush hour. When Caroline wants something more immediate he comes up with the loser having to interrupt William seven times in one day while he is talking with someone else, saying, "William, there's no toilet paper."

William is supervising the cutting of new windows. He has been on the island for six years and has seen many changes, "some good, some bad." Projects get started, abandoned, contractors come and go. Has he ever seen any of Marlon's films? "Yes, *The Godfather* I liked." Does Marlon remind him of the Godfather? "Oh yes, yes he does. Some-times." Does he ever talk to Marlon about it? "No, he doesn't like to talk about movies. If you ever say anything he just changes the subject. But he's a good man to work for, I like him."

Eri, Marlon's cook, has also seen some of her boss's films. "Something in Mexico," she remembers. And "the movie with a trolley. A love story about a man and his wife and her sister. I liked that. He was very young then, slim." She's also seen an Elvis Presley movie once. "He was singing in Hawaii. He was very handsome." Can she distinguish between Marlon and Elvis as actors? "Oh, they're both very nice," she says.

June 20: Day Eight

Gauguin light. Toilet clogged, water off. Another slow day on Tetiaroa.

From my window I see Caroline's daughter, both hands clutching a walkie-talkie with raised antenna making it al-most as tall as she is. She is being led around the island by Marlon, who sits in his bungalow. "Where are you now?" I hear his voice ask. She shouts an answer. "Don't shout," he tells her, "it comes out garbled and I cannot tell you what to do." She whispers back, "I'm not yet at the turtle cage, Marlon."

In the evening Brando and I listen to classical music on cassettes and play chess. He's a bold player and wins every game. "Nobody knows what makes a good chess player," he says. "It doesn't have to do with intelligence, it has to do with a sense of space. Architects usually make good chess players." We screw around, placing pieces at random and playing; then he puts a cardboard shield between the halves of the board and we arrange our pieces any way we want. Removes the cardboard, makes his first move, captures my queen. "Fate's fickle finger has come knocking on your door," he says.

He tells a story about Humphrey Bogart, who played a sadistic game of chess. ("Sadistic," along with "boring," are two of Brando's favorite words.) Once Bogie was set up by some friends who watched him always beat one of the guys on the set. They "wired" the guy and brought in a chess master, who hid in a room above them with a pair of binoculars, telling the guy how to move. As Bogie was losing he got so angry he upset the table and stormed out.

"Being proud is a sickness," Marlon says. "You have to always win, you can never lose. I was like that for a long time. People who always have to win usually have a lot of anxiety, they're very anxious people."

June 21: Day Nine

On an island like this, with little to do, one concentrates on minutiae. A fly walks over my hand, I study its wing structure, its eyes, head, body, the cilia hair on its legs. A mosquito flies by, I notice its black and white stripes. Watch the way a worker uses a broom, the shuffle of his walk.

Notice nature: how the sea moves, the wind bends the palms. For a man obsessed with details, as Brando is, an island heightens that obsession.

We tape until dinner, go night sailing afterwards. The moon is full, Caroline and her daughter join us. We wear bathing suits. Marlon wears a yellow waterproof windbreaker with hood, rubber pants, and boots. Looks like he came out of a chewing tobacco ad. We pull out the Hobie Cat and distribute our weight as Marlon does the sailing. We move fast in the wind. After an hour something on the mast snaps and steering becomes difficult. We pull in.

Back at his bungalow, during our last taped session, Marlon avoids questions about how much pain is involved in being an actor. He'd rather talk about women with big asses, which he prefers to women with small ones. "A woman with a small ass I treat almost as if she's paralytic." He tells me stories about women in his past. One woman plastered his poster from *Streetcar* all over her walls. She'd call him all the time when he lived in an apartment in Greenwich Village. She wouldn't tell him her name for six months, but said that she made her money by robbing people. She told him she and a friend were into cannibalism and they could take him to a place in New Jersey where they would eat him. That was sufficiently bizarre for him to at least find out who she was, so he told her to come by his place. When she did, he opened the door slightly with the chain in place, and told her to put both her hands through the door, where he grabbed them and then frisked her for a gun. When he let her in she took out a wad of bills and asked if he needed money. She was into a heavy Jesus trip and Marlon was her Christ. She was Mary Magdalene. She wanted to wash his feet. "Yeah," Marlon agreed, "I guess I can get into that fantasy." So she did, which aroused him. "I started feeling her body, undressing her, playing with her tits. She got all trembly, started shaking. I got excited and tried to fuck her. I don't remember if I did or not, if I got it in or not, because she was just shaking like a leaf."

Then she got *real* weird. She'd call him, stand outside his door, wouldn't leave him alone. This went on for years. He talked about her to his shrink and got her to go see him too. The shrink said the girl had a "fixation complex" and if rejected she could get violent. She was psychotic and dangerous. Marlon had a friend of his begin trailing her. Once she called him from a phone booth, and he told her he didn't want to see her anymore. The girl, according to his friend's report, started to pound the phone booth, breaking the glass, cutting herself up. Then she went to her apartment, took down all her *Streetcar Named Desire* posters, and burned them outside. She stood and stared at the rubble for a few hours.

Sometimes Marlon gets a vague, distant look in his eyes and stares out at the sea. Questions go unanswered. He says he doesn't have any ambition left, doesn't want to do the major plays, act for the sake of acting. He doesn't feel he has to prove himself. As Orson Welles once said, you don't have to repeat yourself to show you can still do it. The fact that you've done it is enough.

June 22: Day Ten

The plane comes in the morning. Marlon is still asleep. We had talked until 2 A.M. When I said goodnight he walked me to the door, polite, tired, a gracious host.

I fly to Tahiti with Tarita. She gives me a ride to my hotel. I ask her which she prefers, living on the island or in the city. "Here," she says, "in the city. He would like me to stay there. Once I stayed there two months. When he's not there it gets lonely. That's no kind of life."

Tarita acted in *Mutiny on the Bounty* and is still an attractive woman with a strong face. I ask if she'd like to be in more movies. "No," she says. Then, "Well, I would like, but he doesn't want me to. He wants me to stay home and raise the children."

At the hotel I kiss both her cheeks and say goodbye. Wondering if the mermaids will ever sing for Marlon Brando.

THE INTERVIEW

3 / "A Little Shtick, a Little Charm, a Little of Marlon's Eccentricities"

When you were a kid growing up in Nebraska, did you ever imagine you'd wind up as a caretaker of a South Seas island?

BRANDO I knew that when I was twelve. I was taking five subjects, flunked four; took four, flunked four; took three, passed two. So they'd send me to a—what do you call it?—study hall. I'd go read books in the library. They used to keep back issues of *National Geographic*. I always felt an affinity towards this place. Through the years I'd read about it. Then, in 1960, I came down here. It wasn't so much of a surprise, it just sort of confirmed what I knew, or what I thought was here.

How did you discover Tetiaroa?

BRANDO I was up on a hill one day with a friend of mine and I looked out and it was out there. I said, "What's that?" Somebody said, "Tetiaroa." I said, "What's that?" "An island."

"Who lives out there?" "An old woman named Mrs. Duran." "Can you visit the island?" "No, you can't." So I found somebody who knew who she was and took me out here in a boat. Talked to her for seven hours. She was blind and was out here for twenty-five years. A remarkable woman, worth listening to. I regret to this day that I never took her stories down. She told me all kinds of stories, most of the time about Tahiti in the early days, what it was like, about French Polynesia. She had forty cats and dogs and a big cemetery for them. She walked around the island led by a wire—she'd wrap a rag around the wire and walk along. Then she'd come to the tree to which the wire was nailed, take the rag off and walk some more. She was a bright and shiny person. I said, "If you ever think of selling the island, I wish you would think of me." She said, "Well, if that day ever comes, I will." And then the day came when she did. Why she picked me out I don't know. But I just loved it and she knew that I would take care of it and protect it. Well, I don't know if she knew it, but at least she felt that I would.

Did you ever have a moment's hesitation about taking over this atoll?

BRANDO Not at all. I thought, what a wonderful opportunity. You have to get permission to buy land here; you can only buy it from other foreigners. I made the application to buy the land and sat down with the governor. I said to him, "Can you think of any reason why I might not be approved?" He said, "No, Mr. Brando, we're very happy to have you in our community here, we're delighted that you should become the proprietor of Tetiaroa." One day before he left his office to return to France forevermore and become a bureaucrat some-place else, he sent me a telegram that said, "Your permission to buy Tetiaroa has been refused." I figured that's that. When I told Mrs Duran she said, "Of course, you've got to keep trying." I subsequently found out that there were lots of ugly complications behind that. There were people involved who wanted the island and had just found a way to have me refused. So I went to Paris. There were some friends of mine who knew people in the government and they introduced me to them. I told them what I wanted to do, they said okay. I got permission to buy.

Well, it's certainly a perfect place to do this interview— no phones to disturb, no unexpected visitors, no interruptions.

BRANDO   It's very elemental here. You have the sky, the sea, trees, the crabs, the fish, the sun . . . the basics.

For most of your career you've avoided doing any long interviews. What am I doing here?

BRANDO   Normally, I wouldn't do this, I wouldn't have this interview. If it weren't for the fact that Hugh Hefner was a guy who put up fifty thousand dollars to get Russell Means out of jail in South Dakota.

Why was Means in jail?

BRANDO   I can't remember, he's been in and out of jail so many times. They arrest him for spitting on the sidewalk or for having his hands in his pockets, loitering, anything. Hugh put up fifty thousand smackers, committing himself to the Indian situation. I know that he did it because he believed that it was right. It was not just something that he did on some sort of whim. It was a gesture of trust. I was very grateful and beholden to him and I said I'd like to write an article if it would be of service to you, and he said, Yeah. Then it was suggested to do an interview, would I hold still for that? I said sure. But I had some time wrestling with myself to find out what the ground rules were going to be.

And when you found out there'd be no ground rules, did you regret having consented?

BRANDO I've regretted most interviews. Because they don't write what you say or they'll get you out of context or they'll juxtapose it in such a way that it's not reflective of what you've said. And then you can say something in a certain spirit, with a smile, but when it appears in print there's no smile.

That can always be indicated with brackets. But when you do make a rare public appearance, as you did on television with Dick Cavett some years ago, you didn't do much smiling. With Cavett you stubbornly insisted on spending ninety minutes on one topic, Indians, which seemed to make him very nervous.

BRANDO Yeah. He kept asking me questions, kept me uncomfortable. Dick was having trouble with his ratings at the time. He's a good interviewer: bright, witty, intelligent, he buzzes things along. But he blew it in my case, because I was intransigent and intractable and would not answer what I thought were silly questions. Which made his show dull.

You weren't dull when the Maysle brothers made their documentary—"Meet Marlon Brando"—of you with the press.

BRANDO   I was just drunk. It was funnier than hell. They wanted to make a movie out of it. I never saw it. I had the most discouraging experience with the BBC, though. I went on a show that was something like *Tonight.* I was very nervous. All he did was ask me questions about *Superman:* how much money I got and stuff like that. He said, "Were you able to get into your costume for *Superman?*" And I would say, "Well, in 1973 Wounded Knee took place." I just didn't want to hold still for any of the crap questions, but I wanted to be courteous at the same time. They edited the thing so I said nothing. I really looked like an idiot.

Then I went downstairs to talk to seven reporters from the London *Times,* from all the papers. I talked for three hours with them about the American Indian. They all ran pictures of me in my Superman costume and that's all they talked about. Then, once in a while, on the back page, "and . . . blah blah blah blah blah the American Indian." I was appalled. I didn't believe the quality of journalism was such that they were so starved that they would have to go for the buck to that extent. And that the BBC should do that. It was revolting.

But not very surprising. Getting you to talk about Indians isn't much of a journalistic scoop, is it? Not to denigrate what you have to say about that subject, but the fact is, anyone who interviews you wants to get more out of you than a single, social issue.

BRANDO   Yeah, but what a paltry ambition. I know if you want to schlock it up a little the chances are the interview is going to be more successful, because people are going to read it, it's going to be a little more provocative and down the line—get your finger under the *real* Marlon Brando, what he really thinks and all that. But I'm not going to lay myself at the feet of the American public and invite them into my soul. My soul is a private place. And I have some resentment of the fact that I live in a system where you have to do that. I find myself making concessions, because normally I wouldn't talk about any of this, it's just blabber. It's not absorbing or meaningful or significant, it doesn't have anything to do much with our lives. It's dog food conversation. I think the issue of the Indian is interesting enough so that we don't have to talk about other things. But I have the vague feeling that you know where the essence of a commercial interview lies, and what would make a good commercial story wouldn't necessarily be one that would mention the American Indian at all. To me, it's the only part that matters.

But you're aware that there are other parts that matter to us. Your passion is with the Indians, but your expertise, if you will, is as an actor.

BRANDO   I guess I have a burning resentment over the fact that when people meet you they're meeting some asshole celebrity movie actor, instead of a person, someone who has another view, or another life, or is concerned about other things. This *idiot* part of life has to go in the forefront of things as if it's of major importance.

But an entire interview dealing with nothing but the problems of Indians would inevitably become boring.

BRANDO   I'd like to be able to bore people with the subject of Indians . . . since I'm beginning to think it's true, that everybody is bored by those issues. Nobody wants to think about social issues, social justice. And those are the main issues that confront us. That's one of the dilemmas of my life. People don't give a damn. Ask most kids about details about Auschwitz or about the manner in which the American Indian was assassinated as a people and ground into the ground, they don't know anything about it. And they don't *want* to know anything. Most people just want their beer or their soap opera or their lullaby.

Be that as it may, you can be sure that there are many people who are at least as interested in what you might have to say, to pick a random example, to the fact that Marilyn Monroe once expressed a desire to play Lady Macbeth to your Macbeth as to what you will undoubtedly be saying about past and present social injustices.

BRANDO   Look, you're going to be the arbiter of what is important and what you think the particular *salade niçoise* ingredients of this interview ought to be—it's going to have a little shtick, a little charm, a little of Marlon's eccentricities, we're going to lift the lid here and pull the hem of the gown up there, then we're gonna talk about Indians. But there are things that you full well know and are aware of that are important. Food is one of them, UNICEF is another, human aggression is another, social injustice in our own backyard is another, human injustice anywhere in the world. Those are issues that we have to constantly confront ourselves and others with and deal with. Maybe what I'm going to say about it is meaningless or doesn't have much of an input and doesn't have any solutions, but the fact is, if we all start talking about it and look at it, instead of listening to my views on acting, which are totally irrelevant, maybe something could get done.

When I say irrelevant, they're certainly relevant to money and writing an article that's going to bring more readers in. You have to have something as a sort of shill for the readers, so if he gets to page one and he reads about what I think about Marilyn Monroe's thoughts about me, King Lear to her Ophelia, or something as absurd as that, or did she have a nice figure and what do you think about women using dumbbells to develop their busts?—I'm exaggerating to make the point—then people are going to read that, and then they may go on a little further and read something about Indians that they didn't know.

Well, we're finally coming around to some agreement here. You're absolutely right. Did you know Marilyn considered you her favorite actor?

BRANDO   I don't know how to answer the question. [*Mockingly*] "Oh, well, that's nice, my goodness, I didn't know Marilyn cared for me in that respect. . . . Hey, well, she's a remarkable actress, I certainly would have enjoyed . . . ," I can't respond to that, it bores the shit out of me.

Can you respond to what happened to her?

BRANDO No, I don't want to talk about that, that's just prattle, gossip, shitty . . . it's disemboweling a ghost . . . Marlon Brando's view of Marilyn Monroe's death. That's horrifying. What she said about me and what I'm to say about her can lead to the consequence of nothing.

Not necessarily. What if the point of this is to lead to the subject of suicide? What if what I'm really trying to get at is asking you if you ever contemplated . . . ?

BRANDO "What if"—it wasn't that, it wasn't "What if."

How do you know that? You don't know what directions these questions might take.

BRANDO Now you're giving me your *yeshiva bocher,* you know what that is?

It's Yiddish.

BRANDO Your *yeshiva bocher* is Yiddish. That's two Jews under the Williamsburg Bridge. It's the equivalent of the Christians arguing about how many angels dance on the head of a pin.

Okay, we've established your reluctance to talk about non-issue-oriented subjects and my open desire not to try to sneak things by you but to confront you with questions you may not want to be asked. Shall we proceed?

BRANDO I'm not casting aspersions on your effort, because what you do you do very thoroughly and tastefully. All I'm saying is there are money-oriented questions. Those that have the best return are the most controversial, the most startling, the most arresting. The idea is to get a scintillating view that has not yet been seen by somebody, so that you have something unusual to offer, to sell. I just don't believe in washing my dirty underwear for all to see, and I'm not interested in the confessions of movie stars. Mike Wallace had a program, it was an astounding program, some years ago. He got people to come on and talk about themselves. And in just conversation they'd throw up all over the camera and on him, the desk, in their own laps, and tell us about their problems with B.O. or drinking or their inability to have a proper sexual relation with their pet kangaroo. I was floored. I was fascinated with that program. He was wonderful: he's very adept, he likes to play the role of the flashing, incisive reporter. He's a damn good investigative reporter.

There's a sea of people who love, can't wait, to tell you about themselves, all their little tasty bits of information, their exhibitionists' nature, can't talk enough about themselves. I watch these programs on television and I'm just in awe of these people who can't wait to talk about themselves, their families, wives, troubles they had. There was one guy who talked about the operation he had on his penis. [*Laughs*] I was astounded.

Anyway, what people are willing to do in front of a public is puzzling. I don't understand why they do it. I guess it makes them feel a little less lonely. I always found it distasteful and not something I care to do. Did you ever read any of Lillian Ross's Hollywood profiles in *The New*

Yorker? They were mostly quotes of what celebrities said. They just hung themselves by their own talk.

That's what many critics said about you when Truman Capote profiled you in The New Yorker *during the making of* Sayonara, *twenty-two years ago. Was that the piece that turned you away from doing interviews?*

BRANDO No. What I was very slow in realizing was that money was the principle motivation in any interview. Not necessarily directly, but indirectly. We're money bound people and everything we do has to do with money, more or less. Our projects and activities have to do with the making of money and the movement of money. I am a commodity sitting here. Our union has to do with money. You're making money, your publisher's making money, and I suppose, in some way, I'm making money. If money were not involved, you wouldn't be sitting here asking me questions because you wouldn't be getting paid for it. I wouldn't be answering the questions if there wasn't some monetary consideration involved. Not that I'm getting it directly, but I'm paying a debt, so to speak. People look for the money questions, the money answers, and they wait for a little flex of *gelt* in the conversation. You can tell when you're talking, they get very attentive on certain subjects.

Did you feel that way with Capote?

BRANDO No, he's too good a writer just to write sensational claptrap. But he would bend or arrange . . . everybody editorializes. It's inevitable. I liked Kenneth Tynan's review of *In*

Cold Blood, which he titled "In Cold Cash." It was a good book, but if Capote could draw three hundred people to a party, then why couldn't he get them to fight against capital punishment? Because it would have ruined five years of research and his book.

Capote, over the years, has not been very kind when he writes or speaks about you. He feels you keep inventing your concern for various social causes as a form of self-dramatization and a way of alleviating your vague sense of uselessness and guilt. Is there anything to that?

BRANDO   That's an invasion of privacy. I mean, there is something obscene about confessing your feelings and your sentiments for all people to view. And who the hell is interested, anyway?

Don't get too angry now—you know *people are interested.*

BRANDO   I'm not angry. But I think that people are not interested. People are curious. And merchandising and pandering to people's curiosity is something that I don't want to be part of.

What do you think people are interested in, then?

BRANDO   They're not interested in *anything.*

What's the difference between interested and curious?

BRANDO Curious is just sort of passing and superficial, interest means you have an abiding absorption with something, that you're really drawn towards this.

And you don't think anyone has that kind of an abiding interest in you?

BRANDO No.

But people do.

BRANDO How do you know?

Why am I here? If you were Engelbert Pumperdink. . . .

BRANDO You make your mumber. . . . [*Starts laughing*]. . . . You couldn't say Engelbert Humperdinck and I couldn't say "money."

If you were Bobby Darin . . .

BRANDO He's dead.

Or Wayne Newton or whoever, I doubt if I'd be here. There is something about the fact that it's you that says "interest." And some of that is "Abiding interest." People want to know who you are. You don't see this? You have to, even if you don't want to deal with it.

BRANDO No. First of all, you know perfectly well that you don't interview out-of-work movie stars and people who can't get a job. I just happen to be lucky and have had a couple of hits and some controversial pictures lately, but I was down the tubes not long ago. I always made a living but I wasn't . . . I wasn't . . . sought after. I suppose if I hadn't been successful in a couple of movies that I would have been playing different kinds of parts for different kinds of money, and you wouldn't be sitting here today.

You don't think, though, that even when you were down the tubes, as you say, that . . .

BRANDO I've been down the tubes several times.

And no one's wanted to interview you then?

BRANDO You can see it on the faces of the air hostesses' expressions, you can see it when you go to rent a car, you can see it when you walk into a restaurant. If you've made a hit movie, then you get the full thirty-two-teeth display in some places, and if you've sort of faded they say, "Are you still making movies? I remember that picture, blah blah blah." And so it goes. The point of all this is, people are interested in people who are successful.

And in people who will be remembered. Which is why we're talking.

BRANDO I don't know. I think movie stars are . . . about a decade. Ask young kids now who Humphrey Bogart or Clark

Gable was. "Didn't he play for the Yankees?" "No, no, he was a tailbacker at Cincinnati."

So you think the fascination in someone like yourself is fleeting?

BRANDO   There's a tendency for people to mythologize every-body, evil or good. While history is happening it's being my-thologized. There are people who believe that Nixon was inno-cent, that he's a man of refinement, nobility, firmness of pur-pose, and he should be reinstated as President, he did no wrong. And there are people who can do no right. [Black activist] Bobby Seale, for some people, was a vicious, pernicious symbol of something that was destructive in our society that should be looked to with great caution and wariness, a man from whom no good can emanate. To other people, he was a poet, an aristocratic spirit.

People believe what they believe to a large degree. People will like you that never met you, they think you're absolutely wonderful; and then people also will hate you, for reasons that have nothing to do with any real experience with you. People don't want to lose their enemies. We have favorite enemies, people we love to hate and we hate to love. If they do something good, we don't like it. I found myself doing that with Ronald Reagan. He is an anathema to me. If he does something that's reasonable I find my mind trying to find some way to interpret it so that it's not reasonable, so that somewhere it's jingoist extremism.

Most people want those fantasies of those who are worthy of our hate—we get rid of a lot of anger that way; and those who are worthy of our idolatry. Whether it's Farrah Fawcett or somebody else, it doesn't make a difference. They're easily replaceable units, pick 'em out like a card file. Johnny Ray enjoyed that kind of hysterical popularity, celebration, and then suddenly he wasn't there anymore. The Beatles now are nobody in particular. Once they set screaming crowds running after them, they ran in fear of their lives, they had special tunnels for them. They can walk almost anyplace now. Because the fantasy is gone. Elvis Presley—bloated, over-the-hill, adolescent entertainer, suddenly drawing people in to Las Vegas—had nothing to do with excellence, just myth. It's convenient for people to believe that something is wonderful, therefore they're wonderful.

Kafka and Kierkegaard are remarkable souls, they visited distant lands of the psyche that no other writer dared go before—to some people that's it, not Elvis Presley, Franz Kafka.

Do you think everybody has heroes?

BRANDO   They have to have. Even negative heroes. Richard the Third: "Can I do this, and cannot get a crown?/Tut, were it farther off, I'll pluck it down!" Described himself as an unlicked bear whelp that carries no impression like a dam. So he delighted in that. He said, "And because I cannot deal in her soft laws . . . gambol in a lady's chamber," something like that. In other words, the fact that life was denied to him then he would do his best at being bad, he would make a career at being bad. The worst kind of bad you could be: memorably bad, frighteningly bad, powerfully bad. Had he had the opportunity he might have been powerfully creative, powerfully loving, powerfully noble. He didn't have the opportunity because he was twisted and deformed and bitter by that experience. It's wonderfully stated, Shakespeare: "Now is the winter of our discontent/Made glorious summer by this sun of York." People who use their energies negatively or positively, those energies are there to be used and they will apply, somehow.

4 / "Everybody Is an Actor"

You *once said that for most of your career you were trying to figure out what you'd really like to do.*

BRANDO "You once said." There ought to be a handbook for interviewers and one of the don'ts should be: Don't say, You once said, because ninety-eight point four percent of the time what you were quoted to have said once isn't true. The fact is, I did say that. For a long time I had no idea really what it was that I wanted to do.

And you didn't feel that acting was worthwhile or fulfilling enough?

BRANDO There's a big bugaboo about acting, it doesn't make sense to me. Everybody is an actor, you spend your whole day acting. Everybody has suffered through moments where you're thinking one thing and feeling one thing and not showing it. That's acting. Shaw said that thinking was the greatest of all human endeavors, but I would say that feeling was. Allowing yourself to feel things, to feel love or wrath, hatred, rage. . . . It's very difficult for people to have an extended confrontation with themselves. You're hiding what you're thinking, what you're feeling, you don't want to upset somebody, or you *do* want to upset somebody; you don't want to show that you hate them, your pride is injured if they would know that you'd been affected by what they said about you. Or you hide a picayune aspect of yourself, the prideful or envious or vulnerable, and you pretend that everything's all right. "Hi, how are you?" And people look at your face and it's presentable. "And I shall find the face to meet the faces that I meet."

Prepare *a face*.

BRANDO Hmm?

That's from Eliot, prepare *a face*.

BRANDO Yeah, "I shall prepare a face to meet the faces that I meet." So, we all act. The only difference between an actor professionally and an actor in life is the professional knows a little bit more about it—some of them anyway—and they get paid for it. But actually, people do get paid for acting. You have a secretary who has a lot of sex appeal and a great deal of charm and she knows it, she's going to get paid for that, whether she delivers sexual favors or not. A very personable, attractive young man, who reflects what the boss says, he's smart enough to know what the boss feels and likes and wants and he knows how to curry favor . . . he's acting. He goes in in the morning and he gives him a lot of chatter, tells him the right kind of jokes and it makes the boss feel good.

One day the boss says, "Listen, why don't you go to Duluth and take over the department there, Jim, I think you'd do a bangup job." And then Jim digs his toe under the rug and says, "Oh, gosh, I never thought, J.B. . . . gee, I don't know what to say . . . sure, I'll go. When?" And he jumps in the plane and makes a small check after what he's been trying to do for four years—get J.B. to give him the Duluth office. Well, that guy's acting for a living, singing for his supper, and he's getting paid for it.

The same thing is true in governmental promotion or a member of a Presidential advisory committee, if he's playing the power game—'cause a lot of people don't want to get paid in money, they want to get paid in something else, paid in affection or esteem. Or in hard currency.

But there does seem to be a difference between the professional actor, who does what he does consciously, and the often subconscious behavior of the nonprofessional.

BRANDO Well, the idiot tome on acting was written by Dale Carnegie, called *How To Win Friends and Influence People.* It's a book on hustling. Acting is just hustling. Some people are hustling money, some power.

Those in government during the Vietnam war were trying to hustle the President all the time so their opinion would be taken over that of others, and their recommended course of action would be implemented. It was constantly that play going on. Rand Corporation would like all of their views to be accepted, that would make them feel good.

"Oh, we did a lot of wonderful thinking today, the President has adopted our views and is going to implement them on Vietnam."

I can't distinguish between one profession of acting and another. They're all professions of acting.

What about acting as an art form?

BRANDO In your heart of hearts you know perfectly well that movie stars aren't artists.

But there are times when you can capture moments in a film or a play that are memorable, that have meaning, and those moments . . .

BRANDO A prostitute can capture a moment! A prostitute can give you all kinds of wonderful excitement and inspiration and make you think that nirvana has arrived on the two o'clock plane, and it ain't necessarily so.

Are any people in your profession artists?

BRANDO No.

None at all?

BRANDO Not one.

Duse? Bernhardt? Olivier?

BRANDO Shakespeare said . . . poor guy, he gets hauled out of the closet every few minutes, but since there're so few people around you always have to haul somebody out of the closet and say, so-and-so said. That's like saying, "You once said." [*Laughs*] But we know what he said. "There's no art to find the mind's construction in the face." Which very plainly means that being able to discover the subtle qualities of the human mind by the expression of the face is an art, and there should be such an art. I don't think he meant it seriously, that it should be established among the seven lively arts, to become the eighth: the reading of physiognomy. But you can call anything art. You can call a short-order cook an artist, because he really does that—back flips, over and under his legs, around his head, carooms 'em off the wall and catches them. Or people who roll pizzas and throw 'em up in the air. Or a chef being an artist. I don't know that you can exclude those things as art, except you know in your bones that they have nothing to do with art.

But do you know in your bones that you have never considered yourself an artist, both now and at the beginning of your career, thirty years ago?

BRANDO No, never, never. No. Kenneth Clark narrated a television program called *Civilisation*. It was a remarkable series. It was erudite, communicative, polished, interesting to listen to. There was a man who knew who the artists of the world were. He didn't talk about any paltry people that you and I know or heard of. He doesn't know those people. I don't think he'd spend eight minutes addressing himself to Jackson Pollock. Except to show you what art has come to. He talked about great art. And he did not include some of the people that you and I know who consider themselves artists. He certainly didn't refer to the art of film.

But film is reflective of our art and culture. Clark's Civilisation *covered a broad spectrum of history. Maybe in fifty or a hundred years the next Kenneth Clark would include the art of the film.*

BRANDO   Why don't you do an interview with Kenneth Clark and ask him that Marlon wants to know [*laughs*] . . .

. . . is he an artist?

BRANDO   Yeah . . . "Would you talk about the great artists in America today and tell us who they are?"

And let's say Clark answers, Yes, he considers Brando an artist, would that mean anything to you? Elia Kazan has already said that as an actor you are the only genius he's known.

BRANDO   If Kenneth Clark said that I was an artist, I would immediately get him to a neurosurgeon.

Now you're ignoring the authority you've cited. If actors can't be artists, what about movies? Would you consider Citizen Kane *a work of art?*

BRANDO   I don't think any movie is a work of art. I simply do not.

Would you go as far as saying that a collaborative effort can't be a work of art?

BRANDO   Well, the Cathedral in Rouen or Chartres was a collective work, brought about over perhaps a hundred years, where each generation did something. But there was an original plan. Michelangelo's Saint Peter was created by him, but thousands of people were involved in it. Bernini or Michelangelo would conceive a piece of sculpture and then have their students, artisans, knock the big chunks out.

Who is the artist in such cases?

BRANDO   The person who conceives it, and also executes it.

In A Streetcar Named Desire *or* Hamlet, *Williams and Shakespeare are artists, right?*

BRANDO   Yeah.

And can there be artists who interpret those works?

BRANDO   Sure. Heifetz certainly is an artist, for God's sake. He is a particular kind of artist, he's not a creative artist, he's an interpretive artist.

Can singers be artists?

BRANDO   [*Long pause*] No.

Lyricists? Cole Porter, Harold Arlen?

BRANDO   Shakespeare's a lyricist, he wrote many songs. Yeah, I suppose any creative writing. But you get so far down on the scale. You're not going to call the Rolling Stones artists. I had somebody compare them with Bach, that they created something as memorable and as important as Bach, Haydn, Mozart, and Schubert. I hate rock 'n' roll. It's ugly. You have to take it seriously because it's there, it's a manifestation of our culture. I liked it when the blacks had it in 1927.

When it was called jazz?

BRANDO   No, it was called *rock and roll.*

I thought Alan Freed coined the term in the Fifties.

BRANDO   That's not a new phrase. Rock and roll is as old as the beard of Moses.

What about someone like Bob Dylan, who both writes and performs his own work?

BRANDO   There are people who aspire to be artists, but I don't think they're worthy of the calling. I don't know of any movie actors, or any actors. . . . There are *no* people . . . we can call them "artists," give them the generic term if they're comfortable with that, but in terms of great art, magnificent art, art that changes history, art that's overwhelming— where are they? Where are the great artists today? Name one. When you look at Rembrandt, Baudelaire, or listen to the *Discourses* by Epictetus, you know the quality of men is not the same. There are no giants. Mao Tse-tung was the last giant.

If we limit the discussion to the world of film, there are plenty of actors today who bow to you as a giant. You may be repelled by that and say it's all horseshit, but nonetheless it's public knowledge that people like Al Pacino, Barbra Streisand, Pauline Kael, Elia Kazan, give you that label.

BRANDO I don't understand what relevance that has. Chubby Checker was the giant among twisters. I don't know what that illustrates. When you talked before about film being reflective of art and culture, the question went *flaming* through my mind: What culture? There's no fucking culture in this country. The last great artist died maybe a hundred years ago. In *any* field. "And we petty men walk under his huge legs and peep about to find ourselves dishonorable graves."

Shakespeare?

BRANDO Shakespeare. So, we've somehow substituted craft for art, and cleverness for craft. It's revolting! It's *disgusting!* That people talk about art and they haven't got the right to use the word. It doesn't belong on anybody's tongue in this century. There are no artists. We are businessmen. We're merchants. There is no art. Picasso was the last one I would call an artist.

That brings art into this century. I wonder what Henry Moore and Marc Chagall would think of that statement?

Picasso, you know, was as commercial minded as anyone. If he signed a check for less than seventy-five dollars it would be worth more if you sold the signature rather than cash the check.

BRANDO I think that's a wonderful joke. It's enormously clever. That he could draw the outlines of an outhouse and give it to somebody and it's worth twenty thousand dollars. 'Cause it's making a commentary on the obscenity of our standards. He knew it was absolute trash, horseshit, but it's just like a Gucci label. Yeah, it's just a label, a Picasso label.

Well, the Brando label is also highly valued. Are you astounded by the money you get for a film?

BRANDO I don't know how we segued into that.

A lot of artists, like Picasso, who received large sums of money also considered themselves worthy.

BRANDO Are you making an association of worthiness with money? These are hustling questions. It's a disposition to get Brando to talk about these issues, people would like to know. You can always feel when something in the conversation is fertile and it's got a dollar sign on it.

You certainly seem to put down what you do.

BRANDO I don't put it down. But I resent people putting it up.

Where would you put it?

BRANDO It's a way of making a living. A very good way.

Do you like acting?

BRANDO Listen, where can you get paid enough money to buy an island and sit on your ass and talk to you the way I'm doing? You can't *do* anything that's going to pay you money to do that.

You do take acting seriously, then?

BRANDO Yeah, if you aren't good at what you do you don't eat, you don't have the wherewithal to have liberties. I'm sitting down here on this island, enjoying my family, and I'm here primarily because I was able to make a living so I could afford it. I hate the idea of going nine to five. That would scare me.

Is that what bothered you about acting in the theater?

BRANDO It's hard. You have to show up every day. People who go to the theater will perceive the same thing a different way. You have to be able to *give* something back in order to get something from it. I can give you a perfect example. A movie that I was in, called *On the Waterfront,* there was a scene in a taxicab, where I turn to my brother who's come to turn me over to the gangsters and I lament to him that he never looked after me, he never gave me a chance, that I could of been a contender, I cudda been somebody, instead of a bum . . . "You should of looked out after me, Charley." It was very moving. And people often spoke about that, "Oh, my God, what a wonderful scene, Marlon, blah blah blah blah

blah." It wasn't wonderful at all. The situation was wonderful. *Everybody* feels like they could have been a contender, they could have been somebody, everybody feels as though they're partly bum, some part of them. Not bum, but they are not fulfilled and that they could have done better, they could have been better. Everybody feels a sense of loss about something. So *that* was what touched people. It wasn't the scene itself. There are other scenes where you'll find actors being expert, but since the audience couldn't clearly identify with it, it just passed unnoticed. Wonderful scenes never get mentioned, only those scenes that affect people.

Can you give another example?

BRANDO   Judy Garland singing "Over the Rainbow." "Somewhere over the rainbow bluebirds fly, birds fly over the rainbow, why oh why can't I?" Insipid. But you have people just choking up when they think about it or when they hear her singing it. She did a wonderful job. 'Cause it's loose enough to include anything. Over the rainbow. Everybody's got an over-the-rainbow story, everybody wants to get out from under and wants [*laughing*] . . . wants bluebirds flying around. And that's why it's so touching.

Had another person sung that song it might not have had the same effect, there was something about the various elements—a young new talent with an interesting voice—that combined to make it what it was. Had someone else played that particular Waterfront *scene with Rod Steiger—a scene considered by some critics as among the great moments in the history of film—it could have passed by unnoticed. For some reason, that scene worked with you, you brought to it something that a lot of people could identify with.*

BRANDO Yeah, but there are some scenes, some parts, that are actor proof. If you don't get in the way of a part it plays by itself. And there are other parts you work like a Turk in to be effective and . . .

Did you know that Waterfront *scene was an actor proof scene when you were doing it or only now, in hindsight?*

BRANDO No, at the time I didn't know.

Was it a well-rehearsed scene or did Kazan just put the two of you there to act spontaneously?

BRANDO We improvised a lot. Kazan is the best actor's director you could ever want because he was an actor himself, but a special kind of actor. He understands things that other directors do not. He also inspired you. Most actors are expected to come with their parts in their pockets and their emotions spring-loaded, when the director says, "Okay, hit it," they go into a time-slip. But Kazan brought a lot of things to the actor and he invited you to argue with him. He's one of the few directors creative and understanding enough to know where the actor's trying to go. He'd let you play a scene almost any way you'd want.

As it was written, you had this guy pulling a gun on his brother. I said, that's not believable, I don't believe one brother's going to shoot the other. There was nowhere indicated in the script that kind of relationship they had, it's just not believable; it's incredible. So I did it as if he wouldn't believe it, and that was incorporated into the scene. So there is room for improvisation. Some directors, they don't want you to improvise anything—very insecure, or they're hysterically meticulous about things. And some directors want you to improvise all the time.

Many actors cite your performance in Reflections in a Golden Eye *as an example of superb improvisational acting. Did any of that have to do with the direction of John Huston?*

BRANDO   No. He leaves you alone.

What about Bernardo Bertolucci's direction of Last Tango in Paris? *Did you feel it was a violation, as you once said?*

BRANDO   Did I say that once? To whom? [*Laughing*] . . . "as you once said."

What you said was that no actor should be asked to give that much.

BRANDO   Who told you that?

I read it.

BRANDO   I don't know what that film's about.

I read that statement, too. It's hard to believe.

71

BRANDO Because so much of it was improvised. He wanted to do this, to do that. I'd seen his other movie *The Conformist,* and I thought he was a man of special talent. And he thought of all kinds of improvisations. He let me do anything. He told me the general area of what he wanted and I tried to produce the words or the action.

Do you know what it's about now?

BRANDO Yeah, I think it's all about Bernardo Bertolucci's psychoanalysis. And of his not being able to achieve . . . I don't know, I'm being facetious.

No kidding.

BRANDO I think he was confused about it, he didn't know what it was about either. He's very sensitive, but he's a little taken with success. He likes being in the front, on the cover. He enjoys that. He loves giving interviews, loves making audacious statements. He's one of the few really talented people around.

Pauline Kael made some pretty audacious statements when she reviewed Last Tango, *saying it had altered the face of an art form. Did such critical reaction to the film throw you?*

BRANDO I was talking about this before. An audience will not take something from a film or a book or of poetry if they do not give to it. People talk about great writers, great painters, great thinkers, great creators, but you cannot fully understand what a great writer is writing about unless you have some corresponding depth, breadth of assimilation. To some people, Bob Dylan is a literary genius, and that he's every bit and more what Dylan Thomas was. And Pauline Kael, unconsciously, gave much more to the film than was there. You learn an awful lot about reviewers by their reviews. A good reviewer. A bad reviewer you can't learn anything, they're just dummies. But Pauline Kael writes with passion, it's an important experience to her. No matter what they like or dislike, talented reviewers reveal themselves, like any artist.

Jesus, for a moment there I thought you said artist. *Are there any directors you'd like to work with, like Bergman, Fellini, Truffaut?*

BRANDO No.

Have you seen the Japanese X-rated film, In the Realm of the Senses?

BRANDO No.

What happens when you improvise and the actor you're working with wants to stick to the script?

BRANDO If an actor can't improvise then perhaps the producer's wife cast him in that part. You wouldn't be in the film with such a person. Some actors don't like it. Olivier doesn't like to improvise, everything is structured and his roles are all according to almost an architectural plan.

Critics often lean either towards you or Olivier as the greatest living actor. Do you think having done the classics, Olivier's got the edge, or does that matter?

BRANDO That's speculation. Speculation's a waste of time. I don't care what people think.

Do you care, though, when people say you don't always give a hundred percent when you act?

BRANDO Stella Adler, who was my teacher, a most remarkable woman, once told me a story about her father, Jacob P. Adler, a great Yiddish actor who brought the European tradition of theater with him. He had said that if you come to the theater and you feel a hundred percent inspiration, show seventy. If you come to the theater another night and you feel maybe fifty percent, show thirty. If you come to the theater feeling thirty percent, turn around and go home. Always show less than you have.

Have you ever just walked through a part?

BRANDO Certainly. Yeah.

Often?

BRANDO No.

Like The Countess from Hong Kong?

BRANDO No, I tried to do that, but I was a puppet, a marionette in that. I wasn't there to be anything else because Chaplin was a man of sizable talent and I was not going to argue with him about what's funny and not funny. I must say we didn't start off very well. I came to London for the reading of the script and Chaplin read for us. I had jet lag and I went right to sleep during the reading. That was terrible. [*Laughs*] Sometimes sleep is more important than anything else. I was miscast in that. He shouldn't have tried to direct it—do it himself or just write his memoirs. He was a mean man, Chaplin. Sadistic. I saw him torture his son.

In what way?

BRANDO Humiliating him, insulting him, making him feel ridiculous, incompetent. He [Sydney Chaplin] played a small part in the movie and the things Chaplin would say to him. I said, "Why do you take that?" His hands were sweating. He said, "Well, the old man is old and nervous, it's all right." That's no excuse. Chaplin reminded me of what Churchill said about the Germans, either at your feet or at your throat.

Was he that way with you?

BRANDO He tried to do some shit with me. I said, "Don't you ever speak to me in that tone of voice." God, he really made me mad. I was late one day, he started to make a big to-do about it. I told him he could take his film, stick it up his ass, frame by frame. This was after I realized it was a complete fiasco. He wasn't a man who could direct anybody. He probably could when he was young. But with Chaplin's talent, you had to give him the benefit of the doubt. But you have to always separate whatever a man with talent is and his personality, that has nothing to do with it. A remarkable talent, but a monster of a man. I don't even like to think about it.

It was a rather forgettable film.

BRANDO   Movies are very fluid experiences. What turns out, finally, in a movie is very often at odds—much worse, much better, or completely far afield—than that which was intended when you started out. Lousy performances can be shored up and protected and made to appear effective, and wonderful performances can be crippled and made to look awkward. You're always at the mercy of the director . . . and also your own shortcomings.

What about when you direct yourself, as you did in One-Eyed Jacks? *That was a first and last experience for you, did it cure you of your desire to direct?*

BRANDO   I didn't desire to direct that picture. Stanley Kubrick quit just before we were supposed to shoot and I owed three-hundred thousand dollars already on the picture, having paid Karl Malden from the time he started his contract and we weren't through writing the picture. Stanley, Calder Willingham, and myself were at my house playing chess, throwing darts, playing poker. We never got around to getting it ready. Then, just before we were to start, Stanley said, "Marlon, I don't know what the picture's about." I said, "I'll tell you what it's about. It's about three-hundred thousand dollars that I've already paid Karl Malden." He said, "Well, if that's what it's about, I'm in the wrong picture." So that was the end of it. I ran around, asked Sidney Lumet, Gadge [Kazan], and I don't know, four or five people and nobody wanted to direct it. [*Laughs*] So there wasn't anything for me to do except to direct it or go to the poorhouse. So I did.

Was it a completely new experience for you?

BRANDO No, you direct yourself in most films anyway.

Didn't the studio take the film away from you, finally?

BRANDO I kept fiddling around and fiddling around with it, stalling, so they went and cut the film. Movies are made in the cutting room.

Looking back at your body of work, are there any of your films which you aren't at all happy with, which you would like to erase if you could?

BRANDO No.

Would you change many of them if you had a chance to reedit them now?

BRANDO No, I wouldn't want to do that. Good God, one of the most awful places in the world to be is the cutting room. You sit all day long in a dark place filled with cigarette smoke.

Do you always see the final results of what you do?

BRANDO Sometimes you see it in the dubbing room. I've been in the screening room sometimes. Some films I haven't seen. You're bound to run into them on television someplace. One film I liked a lot . . . the only time I ever really enjoyed myself . . . it was called *Bedtime Story* with David Niven. God, he made me laugh so hard. We got the giggles like two girls at a boarding school. He finally had to ask me to go to my trailer, I couldn't stop laughing. [*Laughing*] We both thought it was such a funny script, a funny story.

Would you have liked to have done more comedy?

BRANDO No, I can't do comedy.

Another "can't do" associated with you is your inability or your refusal to memorize lines. Do you have a bad memory, or is it that you feel remembering lines affects the spontaneity of your performance?

BRANDO If you know what you're going to say, if you watch somebody's face when they're talking, they don't know what kind of expression is going to be on their face. You can see people search for words, for ideas, reaching for a concept, a feeling, whatever. If the words are there in the actor's mind. . . . OH, YOU GOT ME! [*Laughing*] YOU GOT ME RIGHT IN THE BUSH. I'm talking about acting, aren't I?

Actually, it saves you an awful lot of time, because learning lines . . . fortunately, it's wonderful to do that.

78

Wonderful not to learn lines?

BRANDO   Yeah, you save all that time not learning the lines. You can't tell the difference. And it improves the spontaneity, because you really don't know. You have an idea of it and you're saying it and you can't remember what the hell it is you want to say. I think it's an aid. Except, of course, Shakespeare. I can quote you two hours of plays and speeches of Shakespeare. Some things you can ad lib, some things you have to commit to memory, like Shakespeare, Tennessee Williams—where the language has value. You can't ad lib Tennessee Williams.

But how does it affect an actor who is working with you if he's got your lines written out on his forehead or wherever? Most actors who act opposite you don't have their lines written nearby, do they? They have to deal with you, your reputation and whatever that may do to them, and then with the fact that they may be a prop for you as well.

BRANDO   It doesn't make any difference. They're not going to see the signs. [*Names a book title*] I just saw a title on the bookshelf. You didn't see me looking for it, you didn't know that I was even doing that. I can do the same thing if I had . . . well, anyway—it's more spontaneous.

For a man who likes to talk, it's a pity that you brake yourself.

BRANDO   I'm fascinated about anything. I'll talk for seven hours about splinters. What kind of splinters, how you get

79

them out, what's the best technique, why you can get an infection. I'm interested in any fucking thing.

But will you talk for seven hours about your career?

BRANDO   Of course not. Not two seconds about it.

But you have, on occasion, talked to reporters in the past about acting.

BRANDO   I was in error. I made a lot of errors and I don't want to repeat the errors. If we repeat our errors then it makes this seem forlorn. There's nothing sadder or more depressing than to see yourself in a series of similar errors.

To alleviate depression, are there any recent films which have made you laugh?

BRANDO   I haven't gone to that many movies. I liked *High Anxiety*. Mel Brooks makes me laugh. They had a Laurel and Hardy festival on television, boy I laughed at that. It went on all night long, I was up half the night laughing.

Was it anything special Laurel and Hardy did which cracked you up?

BRANDO   I suppose Hardy's exasperation with Laurel and doing dead takes into the camera and shaking his head. Exasperatedly patient. [*Laughing*] That's ridiculous.

What about old Marx Brothers films?

BRANDO   No. When I was young they were funny, but I look at them now and it's embarrassing.

How about Kramden and Norton, The Honeymooners?

BRANDO   Art Carney is a marvelous actor. And Jackie Gleason is a really wonderful entertainer. I love to watch *The Honeymooners.* Sid Caesar and Carl Reiner had some wonderful routines. *Your Show of Shows.* God, they made me laugh. They bent me out of shape. They were all funny guys.

What are some of the more important films made in the last decade?

BRANDO   What do you mean *important?*

In whatever sense you think films might be important—significant, meaningful, of social value . . .

BRANDO   I don't know that films are important.

What about a film like The Battle of Algiers?

BRANDO   It was a good film, but whether it was important or not, I don't know.

All right then, besides High Anxiety, *what are some good films that you've seen?*

BRANDO   Let's see, *Star Wars* was fun. Jane Fonda was in a movie with Vanessa Redgrave . . .

Julia.

BRANDO   Yeah, *Julia*. That was a good movie.

What about foreign films?

BRANDO   There's a Japanese film called *Ikiru* that was very touching. Most of the Japanese films . . . *Woman of the Dunes, Gates of Hell, Ugetsu.*

Ugetsu'd if you're rich and famous.

BRANDO   Jesus Christ, Larry. God! [*Laughing*] I love those jokes. I don't know why I always laugh at that dumb shtick. [*Laughing more*] I have a heart attack on that stuff. It's so silly. You don't find many silly comics anymore. Comedians who stand up there and do flatfoot gapes like Willie Howard. Oh, God, he was so funny. What a funny man. The faces he made. I can't think of anybody who made me laugh more.

Who was he?

BRANDO   Willie Howard was a Jewish comedian in New York. I was a kid doing plays there and I'd go see him between the matinee and evening show. Good God, did he ever make me laugh. He had this guy who worked with him who did a double-talk routine—the guy would talk to him in double-talk and he would share the bewilderment of it with the audience and the frustration of trying to get this guy to say something simple. [*Laughs*] Then his partner died and he worked solo. He made funny faces. He was . . . ridiculous. The most ridiculous person I ever saw in my life. I was hanging on the orchestra pit, just roaring with laughter, and nobody else got the jokes. He was playing to me, just because somebody appreciated him so much. There are very few people who are truly silly and have a sense of the ridiculous. He was one such man. I never got to meet the guy. It's always better if you don't know them . . . comics are famously tragic people.

Like W. C. Fields?

BRANDO   I liked W. C. Fields.

Who else?

BRANDO   Richard Pryor, Don Rickles. Moms Mabley, she made me laugh.

Have you ever seen Lily Tomlin?

BRANDO   Yeah. Good God, is she angry, whew. She gives me the impression of somebody incandescent with rage which comes out in this crinkled-eyed smiling face. Acid. She's funny, but all of her humor comes from anguish, rage and anguish, pain. Don Rickles too. Most humor does.

Even Bob Hope's?

BRANDO   Bob Hope will go to the opening of a phone booth in a gas station in Anaheim, providing they have a camera there and three people. He'll go to the opening of a market and receive an award. Get an award from Thom McAn for wearing their shoes. It's pathetic. It's a bottomless pit. A barrel that has no floor. He must be a man who has an ever-crumbling estimation of himself. He's constantly filling himself up. He's like a junkie—an applause junkie, like Sammy Davis, Jr. Sammy desperately longs to be loved, approved of. He's very talented. What happens to those people when they can't get up and do their shtick, God only knows. Bob Hope, Christ, instead of growing old gracefully or doing something with his money, be helpful, all he does is he has an anniversary with the President looking on. It's sad. He gets on an airplane every two minutes, always going someplace. It didn't bother him at all to work the Vietnam War. Oh, he took that in his stride. He did his World War One and Korean War act. "Our boys" and all that. He's a pathetic guy.

What about Woody Allen?

BRANDO I don't know Woody Allen but I like him very much. I saw *Annie Hall*—enjoyed it enormously. He's an important man. Wally Cox is important. Wally Cox was a lifelong friend of mine. I don't know why I put them together. They're similar to me. Woody Allen can't make any sense out of this world, and he really tells wonderful jokes about it. Don't you think it was remarkable that his time came to get his door prize at the Academy Awards and he stayed home and played his clarinet? That was as witty and funny a thing as you could do.

Brando aged five.
© Pictorial Press

Brando in the Fifties.

Marlon Brando in Tetiaroa
during the author's visit.
©1991 Lawrence Grobel

With Vivien Leigh in Tennessee Williams' *A Streetcar Named Desire* (1951). Brando compared the playwright with Shakespeare. © The Kobal Collection

Brando's "I cudda been a contendah" scene with Rod Steiger in *On the Waterfront* (1954). ©Pictorial Press

Being whipped by Karl Malden in *One-Eyed Jacks,* the only film Brando directed (1961). © The Kobal Collection

With Maria Schneider in *Last Tango in Paris* (1973). Hailed as an erotic and revolutionary masterpiece, Brando credits director Bernardo Bertolucci with allowing him to improvise. © Pictorial Press

On the strike line during a civil rights protest in the Sixties.
© Pictorial Press

In custody of a Washington State Game Department agent after a "fish-in" for Indian river rights (1964).
© Wide World Photos

As Don Vito Corleone in
The Godfather (1972).
© Pictorial Press

Gesturing at a press photog-
rapher during filming of
The Freshman (1989).
Brando did a send-up of his
Godfather role.
© London International
Features Ltd.

Marlon and Tarita in *Mutiny on the Bounty* (1962). She would become the mother of two of his nine children, Teihotu and Cheyenne.
© The Kobal Collection

Brando's simple residence, Tetiaroa, Tahiti. Inside the author saw two double beds, books and cassettes on shelves, a bottle of Rolaids, packages of grape Double Bubble sugarless gum. © 1991 Lawrence Grobel

Brando's island, Teti-
aroa, where the
interview took place.
© 1991 Lawrence Grobel

The dining area, with
its dinner log.
© 1991 Lawrence Grobel

A view from Tetiaroa.
© 1991 Lawrence Grobel

Brando embraces Christian during his son's court appearance for the murder of his half-sister, Cheyenne's, lover (1990).
Larry Davis.© *L. A. Times* Syndicate

Wit and Humor certainly wasn't your intention when you had an Indian woman turn down your *Academy door prize for* The Godfather, *or was it?*

BRANDO No. I think it was important for an American Indian to address the people who sit by and do *nothing* while the Indians are expunged from the earth. It was the first time in history that an American Indian ever spoke to sixty million people. It was a tremendous opportunity and I certainly didn't want to usurp that time. It wasn't appropriate that I should. It belonged much better in the mouth of an Indian. I thought an Indian woman would generate less hostility. But those people considered it an interference with their sanctified ritual of self-congratulations.

Do you feel all awards are ridiculous?

BRANDO Of course they are. They're ridiculous. The optometrists are going to have Oscar awards for creating inventive, arresting, admirable, manufactured eyeglass frames—things that hook on to the nose, ones that go way around under the armpit for evening wear. Why shouldn't they? We have the newscasters' awards, we have the Golden Globes . . . they should have an award for the fastest left-handed standby painter who's painted the sets with his left hand at great speed and who has dropped appreciably less paint on the floor while doing it. And then the carpenter's union should have an award for somebody who can take a three-pound hammer and nail two two-by-fours together.

When you were given the NAACP's Humanitarian Award in 1976, you turned that down.

BRANDO   Yeah, I did. I don't believe in awards of any kind. I don't believe in the Nobel Peace Prize.

You did, however, accept the Academy Award in 1954.

BRANDO   I've done a lot of silly things in my day.

5 / "Jolly Jack and the Fijian Dancers"

There's a certain quote comparing women with catching snakes that has been attributed to you.

BRANDO Who in the world cares? Who would want to dignify that claptrap and crap? We'd be all day doing that.

It's a hopeless and useless task. I don't care what people write or what they think. Good Lord, I gave up caring about twenty years ago. The fact is, quite honestly, I haven't read that much. I don't read the stuff. I was really very naive about what the press is about. But they would write all these things I never said or distort in some ways or misrepresent, it used to hurt my feelings. Now, I don't care at all what they say. Those are mostly conversational scavengers who sit around and wait for some slop to fall off the table. If there isn't any, then they invent some. It's of no consequence at all. Just like all questions about acting.

Do you have regrets about many things you've said which have appeared in the press?

BRANDO No. Regret is a waste of time. I don't regret things. There are some things that could have been different but they weren't, so . . . but I don't regret them. One has to accept whatever is and you don't have to accept what is not. Alcoholics Anonymous has a famous phrase: God give us the strength to change the things we can, to accept the things we cannot change and the wisdom to know the difference.

Have you had any involvement with the Women's Movement or with any lobbying for the passage of the Equal Rights Amendment?

BRANDO No.

Any feeling about it?

BRANDO Yeah, it's something that has to pass inevitably and I'm absolutely astounded that the business community has not seen the ERA as an advantage to them, because the intellectual force women can bring to production standards would be very much to their interest. When you consider something like seventy-five percent of the doctors in Russia are women and thirty percent of the judges in Germany are women, we rank perhaps second only to Switzerland with an antiquated view that women belong in the kitchen doing menial chores.

Why do you think certain states won't ratify the amendment?

BRANDO Why do people hate blacks? Why do people discriminate against Indians? Why is AIM referred to as Assholes In Moccasins in South Dakota rather than the American Indian Movement? People have unconscious fears and floating anxieties, maybe guilt, and they will attach themselves like a raindrop to a speck of matter. People have built-in prejudice, they've got hatred piled up in a very neat place and they don't want to have it scattered by logic.

What is it men hate about women?

BRANDO   I think, essentially, men fear women. It comes from a sense of dependence on women. Because men are brought up by women they're dependent on them. In all societies they have organizations that exclude women, warrior societies are famous the world over for that. It comes from fear of women. History is full of references to women and how bad they are, how dangerous. There're deprecating references to women all through the Bible. Just the mere fact that a woman was made out of a man's rib, as a sort of afterthought. Men's egos are frightened by women. We all have made mistakes in that respect. We've all been guilty, most men, of viewing women through prejudice. I always thought of myself not as a prejudiced person, but I find, as I look over it, that I was.

So, you feel guilty about your feelings about women in your past?

BRANDO   Not at all. I don't feel the slightest bit of guilt. Guilt's a useless emotion, it doesn't do anybody any good. A healthy sense of conscience is useful.

Do you think men's attitude toward women will change?

BRANDO Yeah, oh sure. They used to burn people as witches, now we burn 'em with napalm and call them Communists, so I guess that's some change.

What about gay rights? Do you support that?

BRANDO The lack of rights that apply to children are the ones that appall me. That's head and shoulders above any other rights group. Down here in Tahiti, and in many places, children are treated with respect, like small adults without much of a frame of reference. But for some reason we feel superior to children, and we also feel a sense of ownership. Mothers feel about their children the way husbands feel about women. It's *my* kid. Women who are in the Women's Movement, some of them say they are *not* their husband's possession, but then they'll unconsciously refer to their child as a possession. It's exactly the same kind of language they use about their children as they would hate for their husbands to use about them.

A part of you that's not widely known is your long involvement with UNICEF. How long has it been?

BRANDO About twenty years.

What kind of work do you do for them?

BRANDO We've put on shows in Paris, London, Japan, the United States, traveled around the world, done promos. Mainly, my task has been trying to communicate what UNICEF has done, how much the world needs UNICEF, and what a valuable investment children are, and what an enormous deficit they can be if they're not raised properly. Bring a half-sick child into the world and it costs you a great deal more because the child will never become independent, the child will constantly be needing attention. You can't bring him up educationally deprived, physically and morally deprived. In the 1980s there will be some seven hundred million children without enough to eat, with no jobs and no education. It will hit Southeast Asia first. The highest birth rate is Mexico. But Bangladesh now has a runaway population growth.

Have you done any commercials for them?

BRANDO   We do TV spots, film spots, radio. Last year I did six spots for UNICEF.

Does most of the money come from the United States?

BRANDO   Yeah. Other countries are surprisingly reluctant to contribute to UNICEF on a one-to-one basis. Most people don't give. They give because there's a bunch of celebrities around and they're gonna have a night on the town, see a show, have a party afterwards. That's what it's about, it's not about UNICEF. People don't give a hoot about it. If you didn't put on one of those shows then people wouldn't give anything.

How do you get people to give?

91

BRANDO   The best way to get people is to hire the guys that work for the UJA, the United Jewish Appeal. They know how to get the dough. They're really terrific at separating people from their money.

Weren't you once involved in a film made in India that had some connection with UNICEF?

BRANDO   I was there in the state of Bihar during the emergency feeding program. I was with a guy named Satyajit Ray, an Indian director. We were walking along, seeing the nadir of human experience. These children kept coming around and, oh God, the horror. . . . And he was just walking along like he was walking through fields of wheat, pushing the children aside. It's a human obscenity. He said to me, "You don't pay attention to it, you ignore it or you'll go mad. There's nothing you can do." I wanted to film it and show it to people in the United States. I made an entire film, about forty-five minutes. It showed children in the last stages of life, of starvation; little crooked, whimpering things, covered with sores, scabrous from head to foot, lining up to get their food which was brought by UNICEF. I remember this one little girl, she couldn't find a place in her sari to put the stuff where it wouldn't fall through. I saw the lowest stage of human misery there.

Did you ever show the film?

BRANDO   I showed it to a number of people in my home, including Jack Valenti [President of the Motion Picture Association], who was a good friend of President Johnson. I showed it to somebody at NBC. They said that their news department would cover that and I felt that they didn't want any outside contribution. It showed children dying right on camera. One woman offering me a child who was dying, died right on the camera. Children were staggering, falling down.

Did you narrate the film?

BRANDO I was prepared to do that. Jack Valenti tried to set up a meeting with a Presidential adviser to see it, but then at that time I went out to see the Black Panthers, so I guess they couldn't arrange it or didn't want to see it.

Which brings us to the subject of the news media and another one of those "You once saids." This time, the quote of yours is that the media are "oppressively resistant to feeding the truth to the American people, simply because it doesn't sell." Do you still believe—after the Pentagon Papers and Watergate—that we never get the truth?

BRANDO It's all the news that's not fit to print but print to fit. When I say fit, I mean the market. Because there is a market for news, we see that on television: fierce competition between one news program and another that turns into Jolly Jack and the Fijian dancers. They're entertainment shows. The anchormen are trying to hold the line. They tried to maintain integrity, but the call of the dollar was strong, irresistible. The *Today* Show went over to an entertainment program. The ferocity of that competition of who's killing who, who's knocking who down, who's stealing whose points . . . it's terrific. People get yanked out of their jobs if they drop a couple of points. That's the first consideration of the big stations. They have teasers all the way along, telling you to tune in at eleven, a massacre in Wisconsin. The editor picked *that* out as a teaser. Or, if they haven't got anything going, they'll put a tank car explosion in there. It's tailored violence, they have what they call the tasteful frontier of violence.

Wherever you have business and markets, you're going to have to sell what the customers like, otherwise you go out of your store, look down the street, and the other guy's outselling you. They're selling blood and guts and you're selling *bupkis.*

In America, what is decided what you should see and not see is determined by how much money we spend for a product. What you see on television is an exact ratio to what people want. Everybody complains about television, but if they didn't want it, it wouldn't be there. Television, as a capitalistic instrument, panders to people. It has to. But my God, what a glut of mayhem we've seen.

Do you think TV is irresponsible?

BRANDO   Television is not so much irresponsible as it is un-thinking. It eats up anything, this great maw that has to be stuffed with material—they'll throw furniture in there, their clothes, they'll pull off their toupees, anything to keep the machine grinding. All it's about is money, the sponsors buying time.

Actually, television is just an extension of the dime novel. Drama is a refinement of that, of storytelling. Dance, theater, the Balinese shadow stories: people want stories, they want legends, they need to see good and bad presented in a clear way. It assuages the everpresent conflict in everybody's mind about what is good and bad. Because people get so tired of sitting in the in-between world, it's such a relief to see something that's good or for the devil. That's why dramatists who could take human life and present human conflict without a clear point of view don't make any money. People don't want to see that, it's too troubling. People want to see clearly who the protagonist and the antagonist are. That holds true for any drama, any play. And TV does that to people. Endlessly.

Sounds like you've done a lot of watching yourself.

BRANDO I love to look at television, because that's telling me who is watching and what they're thinking. What people think about is reflected on television, because it's all money. If there was no money involved it would not be reflective of people's tastes and needs. Want to know what America is about, look at the religious programs. What a barometer of people's minds and the state of our culture. It's an exact measure.

Is television something to fear?

BRANDO The audiovisual media is the most powerful instrument for influencing people. The instrument of television and its application is going to alter history, no question about that. It has many dangers. They're experimenting here where you can immediately communicate with the program. People don't have time for reflection. If you tell me something, my initial reaction probably would be emotional, and if I had the opportunity to press a button and if that would somehow translate into a vote or an opinion that would influence other people, it could be very destructive, because after a day or two I might have seasoned my thoughts with reflection and found I made some critical errors.

Do you think the media encourages violence or reacts to violence?

BRANDO It's a subtle question. Especially now with terrorism the way it is. Look, we've had more than a hundred derailing incidents, and almost always it's a tank car with flammable substances in it. We had about five major grain elevator disasters in one year. That's put down to coincidence. We're not told they're acts of sabotage. I would assume that the government has gotten together with the news people and said, Listen, don't make alarming stories about terrorists in the United States. But there are plans afoot to counteract terrorism in the U.S.

Do you think terrorist acts can be a means to effect social change, like what happened in Italy with the kidnapping and killing of Aldo Moro?

BRANDO I never thought that terrorism was going to be effective. I can't imagine how you can get somebody, no matter who it is, and kidnap him, make him write poignant letters to his family, plead for his life, torture him like that for a month and then kill him, and expect to get some kind of political advantage out of it. I don't know how that mathematics works. What has it done? The Communist vote was down, the Christian-Democrat vote was up. I couldn't imagine anything less helpful.

Do you think governments engage in symbolic acts to demonstrate their power?

BRANDO   I think the blackout in New York a few years ago was an experiment to show Russia that we can now control energy. It's our message to them: "Here's what we can do if we want to, guys. You better pay attention to this or we'll just come in and turn off your refrigerators." I know that goes against the theory that you don't show your hand, what you've got, but . . . you see the first blackout went from New York to Canada. Then there was a brownout that went into Mexico. That crosses more than one circuit, so . . .

Do you think that the oil crisis we suffered some years ago was a conspiracy rather than a crisis?

BRANDO   I don't know whether it's a conspiracy, but there are enough industrial executives who have gone to jail over the last twenty years for price-fixing and fiddling with and manipulating supply and demand issues, you wouldn't be going wide off the mark if you said they're manipulating us. For example, if the power companies would quit fighting solar energy and quit leaning on the legislatures and get behind it, if industry gets behind it, it can happen. But the oil and steel companies' interests are allied, manufacturers of cars, plastics—which is oil companies—steel companies, metal, rubber companies, they don't want to alter, to retool, it will cost them too much. They say it's going to hurt them, wreck the economy, they're not making enough in profit. The way they piss and moan about their profit ratings it makes you think over the years they'd have gone out of business long ago. *The Godfather* said that a man with a briefcase can steal more money than a man with a pistol.

Do you think big business is way out of control in America?

BRANDO Corporations have no sense of social responsibilities. They tell lies from morning till night. You see advertisements of the petroleum outfits, everybody wants to take care of the environment, so they show you a doe taking a sip of water in a marsh and in the background we see an oil derrick, and EXXON wants us to know that even the doe is being looked after. They give you all this claptrap that Madison Avenue cranks out. There's an art form. Advertising. Making people do what you want them to do, that's what Americans are good at. They can manipulate anybody at any moment. And it makes precious little difference whether we're manipulated by the state, as in Russia, or by big business as we are through advertising.

What about our being manipulated by organized crime? Steve Allen has said that it's so pervasive that you can't buy a shirt, go to a movie, place a bet, go to Las Vegas, without contributing to organized crime.

BRANDO Sure, organized crime exists, no question. Whether it has infiltrated every aspect of our lives, I don't know. They're going to give the military-industrial complex a run for its money. But they don't consider it organized crime. They think it's just business. The other businesses—big business—start wars in the name of right, liberty, and all that. The Mafia says, "That's just a front, what they really want and what they're after is the good goods. It's just money, and they're no different than we are. We have the same objectives, we take better care of our people than they do." I think, quite possibly, that's true.

Isn't there something other than money both kinds of businesses are after? Like power?

BRANDO Money is power. Money translates into guns, in the name of defense, of course. If you have enough money, you can do anything. You can even get a President shot. All you have to do is hire Sam Giancana, Sirhan Sirhan. You can get anybody killed for a can of beer. Hire some dumbo hit man, pay him fifty thousand dollars. You can hire a seventeen-year-old-kid, he'll be out in the streets in two or three years. That's what the Wa Ching did in San Francisco.

Let's talk about the assassinations of the Kennedys, King, and Malcolm X. Do you think it's possible that it was a lone assassin in each case?

BRANDO It's possible, but by no means probable. And certainly, if they had not been killed, there were plans afoot to kill them. For political reasons. No different than Diem or Allende. If the CIA had known that Castro was a Communist they would have assassinated him long before the Bay of

Pigs. They would have had troops fighting on the side of Batista.

Do you suspect the FBI and/or the CIA as having anything to do with the assassinations in the sixties?

BRANDO   They have to be involved in it. It's safe to assume that the FBI is capable of committing murder. When the FBI first started out there was never a force in the world more efficient and better at what they did. But gradually it became politicized, it was reflective of Hoover's jingoistic concepts of the world: Life as it should be in the United States according to St. Hoover. Hoover very cleverly had information on *everybody*. If a politician moved out of line, he could dump some information about some girl that he slept with. They were all intimidated by Hoover. As for the CIA, that got out of hand after World War Two. It was given licenses it was never designed to have. "Termination by extreme prejudice" were the words they used for murder and assassination. They were real words, it was done.

There are certainly enough books out written by former CIA agents to support what you're saying. But let's go back to the Kennedys, King, and Malcolm X. Did you ever meet John Kennedy?

BRANDO   Yeah, it was at a fund-raising affair at the Beverly Hills Hotel. He was table-hopping, as he had to, and he said, "Hello, how are you, nice to meet you"—he didn't say that, but he had his shtick. I said to him, "Aren't you bored to death?" He looked at me and said, "No, I'm not bored." I said, "You've got to be bored." He thought I was being hostile.

Then he realized that he *was* bored having to do that, going around, people gawking at you. Then a Secret Service man came to the table and said, "Kennedy would like to see you after dinner." So we went to his room there and the evening consisted of everybody getting drunk, including Kennedy. Then he told me that I was overweight and I said that he was getting fat and jolly and I could hardly recognize him. We all stormed into the bathroom and weighed ourselves. And then he said, "I know what you've been doing with the Indians, I know what you've been doing." And that was so much for that. A kind of strange interlude.

And what did you think of Robert Kennedy?

BRANDO I think Bobby Kennedy, really, finally, cared; he realized that all of the rhetoric had to be put down into some form of action. That's perhaps the reason they killed him. They don't care what you say, you can say as much as you want providing you don't do anything. If you start to do something and your shuffling raises too much dust, they will disestablish you. That's what happened to Martin Luther King. J. Edgar Hoover hated black people, hated Martin Luther King. If he stayed in the civil rights area, fine, that's just what they wanted him to do: let the Civil Rights Bill pass so we can deal with the Africans and get their raw materials. So Martin Luther King was in service to what the government wanted anyway. But when he got on the issue of the Vietnam War, he was talking to twenty-three million people who were pretty willing to go down the road he told them to go down. That was too heavy. He upped the ante and they didn't want to go that high.

Is that also why Malcolm X was killed?

BRANDO He was a dynamic person, a very special human being, who might have caused a revolution. He had to be done away with. The American government couldn't let him live. If the twenty-three million blacks found a charismatic leader like he was, they would have followed him. The powers that be could not accept that.

Did you ever meet him?

BRANDO No, I'm sorry I didn't, he was a great man. We won't see the likes of Malcolm X again in our lifetime. He was a man of extraordinary talents, capacities, abilities. If he had lived, America would have been far better off. Our consciousness, who we are, what we do, what we intend . . . instead of believing the claptrap that we read about ourselves, and listening to "The Marine's Hymn" and all the romantic jingoistic jargon that we're shook to death with every day.

I'm often amused when I read American history and I read what great things America was going to be, what great things we were going to produce, the magnificent life we were going to have. We were determined to be an impressive and strong nation that needed a lot of people and a lot of land. And all those people who came: Give us your great unwashed. Well, we got all the great unwashed there was. From every prison, we certainly got a lot of scum and dummies. We didn't get the cream of the crop. We got people from the lowest echelons of society who couldn't make it or weren't happy where they were. Or who were taken from Africa, brought to America by chains and turned into animals.

When you were talking about King, you mentioned in passing that the Civil Rights Bill was passed so that the United States could get raw materials from Africa. Is that one of your theories, like the blackout in New York?

BRANDO   Americans don't give a damn about black people. There's just as much prejudice today as there ever was. The interest that America had in creating Civil Rights was purely economic, after the U.S. was confronted with the fact that it would have to go to black Africa with all the colonial countries gone, and they would have to deal with the black man for business deals. You couldn't sit down with a black man in Africa and say, "Listen, we'd like to do business with you," with black Americans being treated like cattle. So they said, "This doesn't really look right, does it? I got an idea, why don't we give the blacks equal rights, let them eat in the restaurants, go to school, and then we'll say, 'We cleaned our plate, now we'd like to do business with you.' " The American government moved to change the laws in respect of black civil rights at the behest of and on the advice and counsel of businessmen who put them in office. If the colonial countries had still been in Africa, there wouldn't be any Civil Rights Act today.

Do you think many blacks would agree with you?

BRANDO I never discussed it with blacks, except Andy Young, by telephone.

Did he agree with you?

BRANDO He said he never thought of that. How could we possibly get raw materials from black Africa when we were burning black people with gasoline in the South?

6 / "Ashamed To Be an American"

Jimmy Carter is the first President to stress human rights. Think he can change human nature?

BRANDO   Carter has done something that no other President has done: he has brought into the sharpest contrast the hypocrisy of the United States in respect to human rights. He's done a great favor to the Indians because you couldn't find a President who'd given them the opportunity to point out the disparity between what Carter says and what actually happens. He's taken up the issue of human rights like the Holy Grail—put the rhetoric in Mondale's mouth and send him off to do Sir Galahad's work. I don't know whether it was oversight or political stupidity, I can't imagine what it was that made him think that he was going to get away with it; that somehow the world was not going to know that we don't have any human rights for Indians, we don't want to reinstate them. The only time I've ever heard him refer to Indians was one time when someone asked him a question about the infiltration of people from Mexico into the U.S. and they called them

105

immigrants, and he said, "Well, outside of a few Indians, we're all immigrants." So I would take that to mean that he dispensed with the Indians because they were few in number and therefore entirely irrelevant. But the fact is that there are about forty million Indians in North and South America. People tend to forget that there are a million Indians in Canada. And Mexico is primarily an Indian nation. They were possessors of great civilizations. Of the five races in the world, they're the only ones who are not represented in the U.N.

Well, we've come this far without really getting into the issue of the Indians as much as you hoped for, so let's begin with . . .

BRANDO Let me ask you why you want to talk about the Indians?

Well, I don't. . . .

BRANDO [*Cracking up, strong laughter. Finally*] It's funny, I was laughing, seeing the words HA HA HA and then your line: HA HA HA. [*More laughter*] That's funny. I love those kind of outrageous retorts.

I hope Indians have as good a sense of humor as you do.

BRANDO People never think of Indians having a sense of humor, but they are the most hilarious people I ever met in my life. They'll laugh at anything. They'll laugh at themselves. They poke fun. They're sarcastic, sardonic, they're funny on every single level. They simply could not have survived without their superb sense of humor.

You've been involved with human rights issues most of your life, beginning with the Jewish struggle for independence, then the blacks' fight for equal rights, and, for nearly two decades now, you've tried to raise the world's consciousness concerning the plight of the American Indian. It is obviously not a passing fancy with you. How did you first become conscious of the Indians?

BRANDO   I read a book by D'Arcy McNickle, a Flathead Indian who had a degree in anthropology from the London School of Anthropology or something, and another book by John Collier, who was then head of the Bureau of Indian Affairs. Then I went to see D'Arcy McNickle in Tucson. I discussed with him Indian affairs and history. He recommended that I see a group called the National Indian Youth Council. So I attended many of their meetings and through that I became absorbed in American Indian affairs.

And through your absorption, what is it that is most shocking to you?

BRANDO   What is shocking to me is that we can consistently try to expunge an entire people from this planet and not have the world know the silent execution that has taken place over a period of two hundred years. And that this government that we live under—which we all say is wonderful and fall to our knees in worship of—has systematically deprived the Indian of life, liberty, the pursuit of happiness, and, at the same time, screaming around the world, like a whistling skank with rabies, that we believe in life, liberty, and the pursuit of happiness. How in the world can we do that at the same time that we're strangling the life out of the only native culture that existed on this land? The American government has shot them, murdered them, starved them, tried to break their spirit, stolen from them, kidnapped their children, and reduced them to rubble. That is what shocks and angers me.

I am *ashamed* to be an American and to see fellow human beings who, if human rights mean anything at all, have every right to the land they live on, and more land than they have. There were ten million Indians according to the *Encyclopaedia Britannica* at the time of Columbus. There are now about a million. They owned all of the United States; they have precious little to call their own now. They were independent; they have nothing now. Anytime a man wanted a piece of land from an Indian, he was able to get it. So they took all the river valleys, they took all the fertile land, they took almost all the forests, they took everything and left the Indian *nothing*. Nothing but memories, and bitter ones at that.

When the government didn't do it militarily, they did it with documents and promises. We lied, we chiseled, we swindled; swindle, swindle, swindle, nothing less than swindle. Swindled the Indian. And we now will say we did not swindle. We *did* swindle. We *did* kill. We *did* maim. We *did* starve. We *did* torture. We did the most heinous things that could be done to a people. We will not admit it, we do not recognize it, it is not contained in our history books, and I want to pull my hair out when I read high school textbooks that deal with the destruction of a people in two paragraphs.

Our relationship with the American Indian is unprecedented in history. There's no country in the world that has made as many solemn documents, agreements, treaties, statements of intention, that the United States has and broken every one of them, and had every intention of breaking them when they made them. No group of people has ever so consistently and cruelly suppressed another group of people as the Americans have the Indians. There were some four hundred treaties written—*not one* was kept. That's a terrific record. Not one treaty! It is outrageous, it's shocking and unfair and a *lot* more important than whether or not I like to get up in the morning, put my Equity card in my pocket, go to the studio and put on my makeup and do my tap dance, going through a day of let's pretend. There's something obscene about that.

With all that has been done to them, what is it the Indians now want from the government?

BRANDO   What the Indians want is very plain: they want their own laws to apply in Indian land; they want an increase in the land base that was stolen from them; they want their treaties recognized. They want sovereignty, hunting and fishing rights, no taxation. They want to pursue their lives as they see fit. They want reinstatement of their economy.

They want nothing more and nothing less than what the Jews have in Israel. We have long, loud and often said people have a right to self-determination, and we stand behind any country in the world that so determines that it is going to be an entity unto itself. We went to Vietnam and killed millions of Vietnamese and thousands of Americans to prove that what we've said was true, we backed it up with force. But we are not willing to offer reinstatement to the American Indian because there's no future in it. We reinstated the Japanese and the Germans because we wanted to be a presence in Asia and Germany. And a lot of Nazis got back into power so that the organization could be created to resist the Russians. But the American government just hopes that the Indian will fade away into history and disappear.

Do you really think the American government would willingly carve up American land and give it to the Indians, establishing a separate country within the United States?

BRANDO   Of course, why not? Drive through the Southwest and you're impressed with how little of the country is used. We probably have the least people per square mile in the United States than almost any place in the world. There's ample room for the Indian to be given back enough land to live on; future populations could be accommodated in that area. There's enough riches in this country so that the Indian could be properly reestablished as a viable community. France gave all of its colonies back; the Dutch, the Belgians, the British. Some of them gave up their colonies screaming, kicking, scratching, fighting; some did it because they read the handwriting on the wall. No Indian has the hope that the *Santa María* and the *Pinta* are going to drive up the Hudson one day and we're all gonna get on it and go back to the jails in England. But it's a very reasonable and logical expectation to assume that America is going to do what every other colonial power has done.

What do you think was the biggest mistake the Indians made?

BRANDO If Indians had joined together and made a concerted effort to keep the white man from stealing their land and decimating their people they could have wiped the people off the face of the earth as soon as they hit Plymouth Rock. But the Indians don't get along with one another. They never thought of themselves as a unified people.

But I'm on the horns of a dilemma, because I am not the spokesman for the American Indian. They have orators, poets, people who were giants, people who are able to talk better than most poets we know that write. Wonderfully articulate people. But they're never asked for an interview in *Playboy*, they're never asked to come on *60 Minutes*. When there's an occasion, they always stick the microphone in my face. I don't know how many times I've said, "Listen, there are perfectly eloquent gentlemen standing to my left and to my right, please ask them, they are Indians, I am not; they know far better than I do why they're here, don't ask me why I'm here." But their editors say, "Go out and get a recording of the fire coming out of Marlon's nose." It's so distasteful to me that nobody gives a *shit*. I've called up I don't know how many magazines, spoken to writers of international reknown, to Senators who head the investigating committees—everybody's out to lunch.

Would you say that Indians have been more discriminated against than blacks were before the Civil Rights Act?

BRANDO It's not an ouch contest.

What about missionaries, have they done any good for the Indians?

BRANDO   The Church has a tremendous debt that it owes to the Indian. The Church was borrowed by the government as a force to so-call "civilize" the Indian. It was simply designed to disenfranchise the Indian, which it did. The Church was in control, they sat in a room and they divided Indian reservations up like pies: Catholics here, Protestants here, you take this, we'll take that, go get 'em boys. And they went in there in force and threw that Bible around with a will.

Had you been born an Indian, do you think, knowing what you know, that you'd be militant?

BRANDO   That's like saying if your aunt had balls she'd be your uncle. I don't know what it's like to be an Indian. I can only imagine. And what I imagine is it's pretty horrible to be an Indian who cares about being an Indian, cares about maintaining himself as an Indian, cares about trying to establish an image of himself in front of his children. I supposed it would make me pretty goddamn mad.

Let's talk about some of your personal involvements. In 1964 you were arrested at a fish-in for Indian river rights in Washington, weren't you?

BRANDO   It was a priest from San Francisco, myself, and an Indian from the Puyallup reservation. They wanted to test whether or not we would be willing to be arrested. We were arrested, but they didn't book us. We went to jail and then they just dismissed us. They got a call from the governor's office or something. Soon after that first fish-in we went to northern Washington and fished there, but it was the wrong place. We just froze to death, I almost got pneumonia. I was dying. Oh God, I was sick. That was my last fish-in.

Then, in 1975, you joined a group of Menominee Indians who had taken over a monk's abbey in Gresham, Wisconsin, in their attempt to get back the deed from land which had once been theirs. Didn't that turn into violence?

BRANDO They were shooting bullets twice a day, in the afternoon and at night. Dog soldiers came and they were fighting it out for close to a month. One guy was shot, one of the vigilantes, a white guy, was killed. I was in there for about a week, with Father Groppi and some other priests. It was unbelievable, people going out with guns and ammunition, lying in the snow and firing at two-thirty in the morning; everybody sleeping, huddled, trying to get warm, bullets flying around. I was up on the roof one time and bullets started sizzling by me, *whheew, whheww*—sounds very funny. The bullets come by before you hear the gun.

Were you scared?

BRANDO No. The Indians were determined that they should get that deed to the land. It was previously Indian land that had just been grabbed. The Church wasn't using it, it was just sitting around in a Catholic bankbook. There were contingency plans to go in with percussion bombs and gas. That would have killed a lot of people because the Indians wouldn't

113

have surrendered, the expression they had on their arm bands was "Deed or Death." They finally got the deed. And then those goddamn Alexion Brothers, the group of priests who owned the property, took it back after everything died down. Those lying bastards! I was right there in the room when they were negotiating. They gave their word that the [abbey] should go to the Indians for a hospital and that the land should be returned to the Menominee reservation. They subsequently, arbitrarily, took it back, broke their word. After the Indians were arrested they said, "We didn't mean that." There was no noise about it then. And the Indians are still sitting in jail in Gresham.

You participated in The Longest March, which began in California and ended in Washington. You flew to Washington and joined the Indians in their meetings and demonstrations. Was it a successful march, politically speaking?

BRANDO The Longest March was not politically motivated, it was a spiritual march. It was an effort on the part of the Indians to have Americans realize that the Indians are not dead and gone, they're alive and here. For the first time you had tribes comingling. The Navahos were there, they very seldom get involved in Indian politics. There was approval from the tribal chairmen organizations, who usually represent a very conservative part of the political spectrum of the Indian world. The March was also designed to kill the Cunningham Bill which would have done away with the Indian and his treaty relationship with the government. That went into the dirt. But it's necessary to go out and continue to oppose and expose that kind of thinking. And to show the entire world what kind of political thinking is alive and well in the American Congress with respect to the Indian. They do want the Indian expunged.

Dennis Banks, the Indian activist, was involved in some kind of shoot-out with the Oregon highway patrol some time ago. His trailer was all shot up and when the police traced the ownership, it was found that it belonged to you. Could you have been charged with aiding and abetting a fugitive?

BRANDO I am not now nor have I ever been a Communist. [*Laughs*] Let me put it this way, I would certainly aid and abet any Indian if they came to me at this time. I had Dennis down here in Tahiti. I invited him to come down, because they were after him.

How long did he stay?

BRANDO About two months.

Did the government know Banks was here?

BRANDO Yeah. Dennis Banks is a remarkable man, he's a man who's got finely honed instincts, lives by his wits, which are considerable. He's the kind of a man young Indians can look to to be inspired by. Russell [Means] is the same.

Why didn't the FBI go after you?

BRANDO The Justice Department didn't see a practical way of indicting me because it would have inflamed the issues and gotten a lot of coverage. For Russell Means to be thrown in jail is one thing, but for me to be put under indictment for "aiding and abetting" an American Indian who was forced to go underground due to political pressure—the entire thing was fraught with a very special kind of concern that it did not get too large.

Had the people in Wounded Knee been black or white they would have had them dead within twenty minutes. You would have seen something that would have made the S.L.A. shoot-out look like a strawberry festival. But they couldn't do it. The only reason they didn't do it was not for any humanitarian reasons, but because the silhouette of the American Indian around the world was so great, Hollywood has made the American Indian famous. The American Indian has been the bread and butter of Hollywood from time immemorial, since its conception. If they shot all those Indians, gassed them, and had these APCs— armored personnel carriers—go in there, we'd of had a shooting war. A lot of Indians would have gone to their death. Then you would have had a black eye in front of the world that the United States couldn't get rid of for a long time. They didn't give a shit about killing people, they simply didn't want to have to put up with the image of the U.S. grinding the life out of a few Indians who were fighting for their land and their way of life. It just contradicted everything that America says it stands for.

When did you come to feel that, second only to the government, Hollywood has done more harm to the American Indian than any other institution?

BRANDO I can't give you a date when the light bulb went off in my head. I became increasingly aware just recently of the power of film to influence people. I always enjoyed watching John Wayne, it never occurred to me until I spoke with Indians how corrosive and damaging and destructive his movies were. Most Hollywood movies were.

Have you ever discussed this with Wayne?

BRANDO I only saw John Wayne once. He was at a restaurant. He came over, very pleasant, wished us all a good evening and a happy meal and walked away. First and last time I saw him.

John Wayne told Playboy *that he didn't feel we did wrong in taking America away from the Indians. He thought the Indians were "selfishly trying to keep it for themselves" and that what happened in the past was so far back that he didn't feel we owed them anything. Care to comment?*

BRANDO That doesn't need a reply, it's self-evident. You can't even get mad at it, it's so insane that there's just nothing to say about it. He would be, according to his point of view, someone not disposed to returning any of the colonial possessions in Africa or Asia to their rightful owners. He would be sharing a perspective with Mr. Vorster if he were in South Africa. He would be on the side of Mr. Ian Smith. He would have shot down Gandhi, called him a rabble rouser. The only freedom fighters that he would recognize are those who are fighting Communists; if they were fighting to get out from under colonial rule, he'd call them terrorists. The Indian today

117

he'd call agitators, terrorists, who knows? If John Wayne ran for President, he would get a great following.

Do you think his views are prevalent in Hollywood?

BRANDO Oh sure, I think he's been enormously instrumental in perpetuating this view of the Indian as a savage, ferocious, destructive force. He's made us believe things about the Indian that were never true, and perpetuated the myth about how wonderful the frontiersmen were and how decent and honorable we all were.

Besides Wayne, you've been outspoken about the insensitivity of many of the Jewish heads of studios, who were in power during the heyday of the cowboy-and-Indian pictures. What made you so angry?

BRANDO I was mad at the Jews in the business because they largely founded the industry. The non-Jewish executives you take for granted are going to exploit *any* race for a buck. But you'd think that the Jews would be so sensitized to that that they wouldn't have done it or allowed it. You've always seen the wily Filipino, the treacherous Chinese, the devilish Jap, the destructive, fierce savage, blood-lusting, killing buck, and the squaw who loves the American marshal or soldier. You've seen every single race besmirched, but you never saw an image of the kike. Because the Jews were ever watchful for that—and rightly so. They never allowed it to be shown on screen. The Jews have done so much for the world that, I suppose, you get extra disappointed because they didn't pay attention to that.

Was there any Jewish reaction to what you've said about the Jews in the movie industry?

BRANDO   No. You have to be very careful about that issue, because the blacks are concerned about the blacks, the Indians are concerned about the Indians, the Jews are concerned about the Jews. In the United States, people are trying to look out for their own. The Puerto Ricans are not going to take up the Indian cause. The Indian cause is not going to be concerned about the injustice to the Japanese. Everybody looks to whatever's close at hand.

Your Indian interests border on an obsession, but then you seem to always get deeply involved with causes you are stirred by. Not many people know of your strong involvement with the creation of the state of Israel and your support of a Jewish terrorist group. How was your consciousness raised at that time, during the late 1940s?

BRANDO   I was, in a sense, brought up by Jews. Stella Adler was the first woman, first person of culture, that I ever met. I was just a kid from Nebraska with a red hat and no idea of how the world was run. As a result of meeting Stella, her daughter, and her husband, Harold Clurman, I met a lot of people in New York and became aware of things that I would never normally have been aware of. I was in a play by Ben Hecht called *A Flag is Born*. It was a pageant to raise money for the Irgun Zvai Leummi. It was actually the League for Free Palestine and we were trying to raise money to buy arms and ammunition and influence to bring in the Zionists and not the Palmach, because that was under Ben-Gurion and they weren't doing as they should have done. We went around the country visiting temples, one Jew and one non-Jew, doing the play. Paul Muni was in it. We went around arguing with these old cockers about why they should not further support the Haganah but should support the Irgun. We collected what money we could and sent it back. So I was involved on the ground floor when all that shit was going on. We had to take a six weeks' course and learn about Israel and how it was formed, how it became a state, the Balfour Declaration and the presence of the British, the position of the Arabs.

And what do you think of now with what's happening in the Middle East? Do you think there's been a rise in anti-Semitism lately?

BRANDO Anti-Semitism? I used to have to ask people what that was. I didn't understand the word. I could never figure it out. It's still a problem to figure out. The Jews have made a far greater contribution to the world of progress, enlightenment, than any other single people. Far and away the Jews have contributed to art, culture, science, literature, the professions, goods and services, law, the advancement of jurisprudence, economics. It's phenomenal. And, almost rightly so, one should say they are the Chosen People. But that impresses nobody. In spite of what good people do, in spite of what happened in Germany, an unprecedented event in world history, there is anti-Semitism. I've run into it I don't know how many times. Casual.

In The Young Lions *you portrayed a sensitive, multidimensional Nazi officer, which upset Irwin Shaw, whose novel*

120

it was based on. Didn't you once agree to debate Shaw about the nature of the German character?

BRANDO   Yeah. He felt that the German people were to blame for the Holocaust. I think if you hold an entire people responsible for something, nobody can survive. Whether it's the Turks, the French in Algeria, the English in Africa and Palestine, the Americans, Spanish—there isn't any people in the world that hasn't done something that defies one's sense of horror. You could say all the Indians in India are responsible for the condition of the Untouchables, all the Japanese are responsible for the condition of the Eta or the Ainu. The Australians used to hunt the Aborigine people and still treat them as something less than human. If you pick out a whole people and say, *all* the Germans are this, *all* the Jews do this, that's exactly what Hitler did. If you start thinking and feeling in broad terms like that then it's very dangerous. That was clear in Shaw's book, in his bitterness and anger. It's fully understandable. But he wanted to make that massive statement. I don't think it's possible to do that.

Just as it's not possible to accurately depict the Indians on film.

You once mentioned two films—Broken Arrow, with Jeff Chandler, and John Ford's Cheyenne Autumn—*as not having treated Indians negatively. Are there any others you can add to that?*

BRANDO   Not *Cheyenne Autumn*. That was worse than any other film because it didn't tell the truth. Super-duper patriots like John Ford could never say that the American government was at fault. He made the evil cavalry captain a foreigner. John Ford had him speak with a thick accent, you didn't know what he was, but you knew he didn't represent Mom's American pie. And it was *his* fault—the torturing of the Indian men, women, and children, letting them freeze in temperature fifteen below zero, not giving them any water. Of course, the truth is that it was a decision made in Washington that reduced one hundred twenty-three people to rubble. There were six of them, wounded, left, who charged the cavalry with knives. That was all they had left in the snow.

Do you approve of any of the films Hollywood has made about the Indians?

BRANDO I can't think of any off hand. I keep thinking of John Wayne. I saw *Hondo* on television the other night. The Indians, of course, are always represented as savage, vicious, destructive, torturing, monstrous people. He has no sense of social responsibility to the Indian children whose characters are being forged watching that thing. I don't know whether it's out of ignorance or what that persuades the man to depict people that way. Maybe he doesn't realize the damage.

On the more positive side of Indian portrayals, what about a film like Soldier Blue?

BRANDO Oh yeah, with Candice Bergen. That film left a lot to be desired, it dealt more with blood and guts than the philosophy, which is important. It was certainly horrifying—

the attack on Sand Creek, when they slaughtered the Indians. In many ways that was representative of what happened.

What about Richard Harris in A Man Called Horse?

BRANDO   That had nothing to do with politics, with the white man and the Indian. There were parts of *Little Big Man* that I thought were useful. It had a lot of good, fair things in it.

I imagine you expect to have a lot of good, fair things in The First American, *the TV project you've agreed to do for ABC. It's your first venture into television, can you talk about it?*

BRANDO   We've been given a chunk of money to do as many programs as we can on that. Hopefully we're going to get four programs out of it. If they like them, they will do more. We're certainly going to work as hard as we can to make them interesting, provocative and truthful. These issues are going to be clearly drawn so that people can't duck them anymore. The Indian view will be heard, and it will be heard round the world. I'll take it to every country, I'll get arrested, I'll give them a show, I'll entertain them, people will say, "Where's Marlon been arrested this time?" I'm totally committing myself to getting this issue across.

How are you researching it?

BRANDO   We've been on the road, listening to ancient and modern horror stories, looking at old sites, running down the facts of history, remembrances of people, going to places where there were battles. In one massacre they cut off women's vulvas and wore them as hat bands.

How are you going to show that on television?

BRANDO   You can't. But there are other stories, of Indians getting arrested and assassinated in jail, then calling it suicide.

How long will each show be?

BRANDO   An hour and a half. Hopefully there's gonna be thirteen or fourteen made. We shouldn't have to go around, hat in hand, scratching and tapping on doors, climbing over transoms, to get money to do a historical survey of the American Indian and how we reduced him to rubble. Jesus Christ!

Will you act in every show?

BRANDO   I will be in a number of them. So far I see myself in one of the four, and I'll probably be in another.

Is it your intention to play figures like Kit Carson and Custer?

BRANDO   I'm too old to play Kit Carson, and Custer. Kit Carson was a relatively young man, most of those guys were. You can cheat twenty years . . . but there are a lot of people I could play.

Well, if they could turn Dustin Hoffman into a hundred-year-old Indian in Little Big Man . . .

BRANDO   Oh, I've played a seventy-year-old man—you can go older, but it's very hard to go younger. Loretta Young finished her days in a blaze of ectoplasm, along with the number of silk screens that they had to put on the lights to soften them so her wrinkles wouldn't interfere with the fun.

Will The First American *be commercialized, as* Holocaust *was, or will you have some control over the way it's presented?*

BRANDO   *Holocaust* was as obscene as anything I've seen on television. I was infuriated by that. It made me gag. I was embarrassed for the people who did it, it was horrifying! Elie Wiesel, who was a man who survived Auschwitz, came out and broadsided the program. That should be treated sanctimoniously as an event in history, it should not be sandwiched between some dog-food ads. How can you go from a concentration camp scene to a smiling woman selling dog food? God! It was appalling. Finally, it's better that they put that on than nothing. But I was talking to one executive who . . . oh, to hell with it.

No, don't stop there.

BRANDO   My argument with television is they will not spend the money to get the qualified people. Very few people will go on television, dramatic TV, if they're actors; very few producers once they've gotten out of TV will go back. Because the quality of production is so poor that they just don't want to be associated with it. Businessmen have control over so-called artistic considerations and they just make formulas. There are morality plays: the good is totally good and the bad is totally bad, and at the end of the half hour you go away smiling and the pimp or the pusher or the mad-dog killer has been put away. The fact is that money is the god-king, the god-head. And we're made to feel that in America. And our culture reflects it: The impoverished standard of the arts, a fatality of hope . . .

What would give TV competence is if the people of quality would do it—writers, actors, directors. Because, finally, they pay for that anyway. If they want to get a film that they consider to be good, *Star Wars* or something like that, they won't make *Star Wars,* because they don't have enough confidence, they're not a production company, they produce television shows. They wait for some movie, like *Jaws,* and then they will buy it for one showing for ten million dollars. After it's done. They don't want to stick their foot out, 'cause television executives are about as expendable as bottle caps.

Well, your instincts seem to have given precedence to television over film. You're going to play the part of American Nazi leader George Lincoln Rockwell, in the second half of Roots. *What made you want to play him?*

BRANDO Everybody ought not to turn their backs on the phenomenon of hatred in whatever form it takes. We have to find out what the anatomy of hatred is before we can understand it. We have to make some attempt of putting it into some understandable form. Any kind of group hatred is extremely dangerous and much more volatile than individual hatred. Heinous crimes are committed by groups and it's all done, of course, in the name of right, justice. It's John Wayne. It's the way he thinks. All the crimes committed against Indians are not considered crimes by John Wayne.

Will you play Rockwell as an evil character?

BRANDO I don't see anybody as evil. When you start seeing people as evil you're in trouble. The thing that's going to save us is understanding. The inspection of the mind of Eichmann or Himmler . . . just to dispense with them as evil is not enough, because it doesn't bring you understanding. You have to see them for what they are. You have to examine John Wayne. He's not a bad person. Who among us is going to say he's a bad man? He feels justified, what he does. The damage that he does he doesn't consider damage, he thinks it's an honest presentation of the facts.

Is what interests you in doing Rockwell to point out that he may not be very different from any of us?

BRANDO We have to examine what he says, what he thinks and what he believes. Then we have to make it known.

Will you try to play him the way he actually was when Alex Haley interviewed him?

BRANDO No, you can't do imitations of people, they never work.

Did you ever consider that you might be glamorizing a guy like Rockwell by agreeing to play him? So that the nuts out there who may watch it will think, hey, I can get Marlon Brando to play my life, all I have to do is outdo Rockwell.

BRANDO You do that by printing the interview with John Wayne, printing his opinions about how justified we were. He can influence an awful lot of people against the Indian, who say, "Damn right, we should have killed 'em, they were right when they said the only good Indians are dead Indians." Yeah, there are people out there who are just waiting for that kind of justification and John Wayne gives them that to hate and be destructive towards Indians.

That still doesn't answer the question of how you justify in your mind playing such a character?

BRANDO Under the rug is worse than on top of the rug. If you sweep something under the rug and say it didn't happen— that was the view during Watergate. Ford made the decision to pardon Nixon because he thought the country could not afford to show the world the level of the depths we had sunk with Nixon.

So your motivation is to understand prejudice, shed light on the darker parts of souls like Rockwell?

BRANDO Understanding prejudice is much more helpful than to just condemn it out of hand. There is a point, however, where you can understand so much and then you've got to take a gun out and say, "I'm not gonna let you do this to me anymore, if you do that I'm gonna kill you." If somebody came to my house I'm going to do damage. I'd kill somebody. I wouldn't hesitate.

You say that, but the act of actually doing it is something else.

BRANDO I've pointed guns at people. Loaded guns.

Did you have your finger on the trigger?

BRANDO Damn right I did. I've told people to get down, lie on the floor, frisked them, got their identification.

When they break into your house?

BRANDO You betchya.

Did any intruder ever not *lay down immediately?*

BRANDO No. Three or four times I've pulled a gun on somebody. I had a problem after Charles Manson, deciding to get a gun. But I didn't want somebody coming in my house and committing mayhem. The Hillside Strangler victims—one of the girls was found in back of my Los Angeles house. My next door neighbor was murdered, strangled in the bathroom. Mulholland Drive is full of crazy people. We have nuts coming up and down all the time.

Do you get a lot of hate mail?

BRANDO Not a lot. I've gotten some threatening letters.

Do you give them to the FBI or are you under surveillance by them for other reasons?

BRANDO Jack Anderson got some stuff from the Secret Service which had me on the list of those who had to be put under surveillance every time the President came to town. Back in the Sixties there was a municipal Department of Water and Power truck parked in front of my house, around eleven at night. I said to them, "What's going on?" "Oh, just fixing the lines." I happen to know something about electricity so I asked some questions, and the guy in charge didn't know and gave me dumb answers. I've had the FBI visit me on five occasions, asking me a lot of questions.

Which probably gave you some good material for that movie you've wanted to do about Wounded Knee. What's happened to that project?

BRANDO I have a very specific notion to make a film out of Wounded Knee to show the FBI and the Justice Department bureau and how what happens to Indians happen, and the way the mind of the politicians work in respect to the Indian. I think it would make a very good movie. It would start with the trial of Banks and Means and keep flashing back to how it happened.

Didn't Abby Mann, who wrote Judgment at Nuremberg, *do a script for you?*

BRANDO He did three scripts.

Were any of them close to what you wanted?

BRANDO   Hardly. Really bad scripts.

And wasn't Martin Scorsese going to direct, until he had problems with the Indians?

BRANDO   Yeah. The Indians don't take anybody's word for anything. They want to find out who you are in their own way. The Indians have revived an asshole concept of who's a warrior and who isn't, like the blacks after the Civil Rights movement. The macho black had his masculinity taken away from him and he was anxious to get it back and state it loud, 'cause it feels good. Well, the Indians have that. So, somebody made a pass at his [Scorsese's] girl, or his girl made a pass at somebody—one of those dumb things—and he didn't do any-thing about it, he didn't give a shit about the girl, what the fuck does he care? Well, a man who doesn't fight for his woman can't be a man we want to have direct our movie, so they shot him down.

Did you have anyone else in mind to direct it?

BRANDO   I tried to get a guy I did a movie with before, Gillo Pontecorvo. He did *The Battle of Algiers.* I thought he'd be perfect for this movie. I was in another movie with him, almost fucking killed him, and he almost killed me. Good God, what a battle that was.

That was Queimada *or* Burn!

BRANDO   Yeah, *Queimada,* which I thought was a wonderful movie. Jesus, they couldn't flush it away fast enough. I couldn't believe it, about an interesting time well told.

Why was it flushed away so fast?

BRANDO I don't know. They let it die, it never appeared anyplace, as though it got the plague or something. Very mysterious. Anyway, Gillo came over and went up there and they scared him to death. Bunch of guys met him at the airport, with about half a bag on, scared the shit out of him. He came back, didn't know what was going on. I told him, he won't understand for a long time what the Indians are—they're very strange folks. And he was going along with it. And then he wanted Franco Solinas, a full-fledged Marxist, to write the script. And it was then the Indians backed off and said, "Nothing doing, we're not going to have a goddamn Communist writing our story." So that was the end of that.

7 / Extraordinary Men, Devil's Fingers, and the Inside of a Camel's Mouth

What really happened when you worked with Ponte-corvo, was it just a true conflict between director and actor?

BRANDO   No, the guy was a complete sadist. He did an awful thing, he wanted to pay the blacks, and did pay the blacks, a different salary than he paid the whites for the same extra work on the grounds that the whites wouldn't work with the blacks in Cartagena [Colombia] at the same salary. Then they gave the blacks different food because they thought they'd like it. Well, the blacks piled up the food against the camera one noon.

I said I wanted some decent food, because the guys were eating shit out there, the crew and the black extras. So the guy made a big to-do about it. They sent out a waiter in a red coat with a white napkin over his arm, prepared a table outside—which I knew they were going to do to try and humiliate the capitalist movie actor. So I said, "There's a spot on the glass." They cleaned that off. Everything was all set up, and the waiter was there, and they were all standing around waiting to snicker, they had a little sunshade for me. I said, "Okay, where's the food?" Made a few suggestions about the food, salt, and I don't know, the wine wasn't cold enough. And then I got the poorest blacks who were on the thing and I let them sit down and I served them. They didn't think I was going to do that and it really blew 'em off.

And there were incidents. He kept these guys kneeling in one position for eight hours in black uniforms, in the sun, eleven degrees from the equator.

The crew was rebelling. The cameraman got a sty in his eye, somebody got a heart attack, somebody else got an ulcer. It was *horrible*.

So, what did you do?

BRANDO   I started out saying, "Jesus Christ, Gillo, you can't pay the blacks different money, you've got to give them the same food, what the fuck, black journalists are coming down here, you think they're gonna hang around here ten minutes without talking to the blacks and find out what the fuck's going on?" I said, "I'm not gonna take the fall for that, god-damnit, you can't do that, that's what this picture's about." I went raving on. Fucked around, how Evaristo [Marquez] was going to walk off the picture, the black guy. His brother was working as an extra, getting shitty food.

Then there was a big mob scene. I'm supposed to meet Evaristo with the head of the revolutionaries. We meet on the beach, our horses mill around each other and we talk. People in the village come to greet Evaristo and the army, which is victorious, and they crowd around and there were

134

a lot of children. So we rehearsed it and the crowd came and they pushed right against the horses. I saw kids running underneath the horses, and the horses were frightened. After the rehearsal was over I went over and said, "For Christ's sake, Gillo, do you know that the children were there, you could get somebody killed here? These are not movie horses." He said, "Oh, yeah, yeah, what's the matter, why did the horses . . . ," you know, the Italians always talk bullshit. So, it was all taken care of. The next one was a take, and they did exactly the same fucking thing. He hadn't told them anything. So I just rode off and said, "I'll be back for the close-up."

Then he also wanted me to say a line in a certain way and I wouldn't do it. So he did forty-nine takes. He tried to get me to blow up, he tried to get me to do it. I had a friend of mine go out and buy me one of these stools. It was a close-up.

I took the stool and I tied it to my ass and then read a magazine sitting down. Then when he'd say, "Okay, ready," I'd stand up and I'd do the scene, and then he would say, "Cut, cut." Then I'd sit down and start reading, through forty-nine takes. He's the most hysterical person I've ever met. As a director he makes you act on a razor's edge all the time. But he has an undercurrent of sadism that doesn't appear. He's enormously sadistic.

Did you ever finally have it out with him?

BRANDO One day, he had me do so many takes on this thing, I just blew fucking up. *Screamed* at the top of my lungs, "You are eating me like ants!" [*Laughs at the memory*] He jumped off the floor about four feet. I could have broken glasses if there'd been any around. I didn't know I was going to do it, it just happened.

There were so many horror stories with that film. I came to the set one day, on location on this mountain road, and the wardrobe woman was sitting near the camera and she had a kid. I said, "What's the matter with the kid?" She said he was sick. I said, "What's the matter?" "Well, he vomited a worm at lunch." I said, "He vomited a worm?" She said, "Yeah, he's got a fever." I said, "Where's the doctor?" She said, "We're going to take him to the doctor after the next shot." I said, "Take him now!" She said, "Gillo wants to finish the scene first, then that will kill the location." So I called out and had the chauffeur come up and I said, "Take the kid to the fucking hospital right now." I really got steamed. If Gillo had been taller I would have fucking fought with him. I really would have punched the guy out. I just looked at him. He said something and I got in the car and went home.

What about the crew, did they ever rebel?

BRANDO   Finally, the crew went on strike. For three months they'd been getting four or five hours sleep. They gave me a little plaque at the end of it. Because I left, and I would not go back to Cartagena. I just walked off the picture finally. People were just dying. I said, unless they finish the picture in Africa, I'm not coming back. So they said, "Okay, come back and we won't sue you." I said, "Gillo, I want you to write me a letter of apology so I could have it on record, and also I want you to tell me we're going to Africa, otherwise you'll have to sue me." Well, I didn't have any money at that time, and they knew fucking well I didn't have six million dollars, which is what the picture was costing. They were not interested in winning a lawsuit, they were interested in getting a picture done. So I had 'em by the nuts. They went to Africa, all the guys went home, half the crew left, went back to Italy. See, in Italy, it's so small that if you don't play ball then you don't work, they won't call you. The management really has full control over the situation.

So, after all this happened, how was Pontecorvo to work with?

BRANDO   He started carrying a gun. Finally sent word to me that he was going to use it if I didn't do what he said. He laughed, but he actually had a gun on his belt. He was very superstitious, hysterically superstitious. On Thursdays you could not ask him any questions. He could not say no to any requests, so nobody could talk to him on Thursday. He would not have one bit of purple. If there was *anything* purple on the set, he would get it off. If somebody spilled wine at lunch, he'd have to go around to *every* person and do this [*makes a gesture*]. So, I had him over a barrel. First day of shooting, we're in a room in a castle in Cartagena, looking down on the square, where this guy is being garroted. We're in a tiny little room, shooting through cell bars on down the courtyard. And he's dressed in an overcoat. Inside that room the temperature is one hundred thirty, one hundred forty. They have great big lights in there. And he has an overcoat on. I said, "Gillo, what are you doing with the overcoat, why don't you take it off?" He said, "No, no, it's all right." I said, "Have you got a cold?" I found out from somebody it's his good luck thing, that he always does it. And then I found out that the prop man has to play the first part in every picture. And that the prop man has to wear certain tennis shoes in all his pictures. And that he has to print a certain take.

He had these two pockets full of plastic charms, devil's fingers, funny-shaped things to ward off evil. He was looking for something and he pulled out these things, and I said, "What's that?" He said, "No, nyente, nyente." Finally he told me they were just good luck pieces. But he was dead fucking serious about that. So, near the end I'd open the door and I'd take a big mirror and say, "Hey, Gillo," and I'd take a hammer and go *whoom, whoom*. [*Laughs*] I walked under ladders. I had him fainting, staggering, just hanging on the ropes. I would spill salt all over the place, throw it around, on the ground. I took some wine at lunch one time. He was trying to bullshit with me, he treated me like one would treat Burt Reynolds—I don't know why I've got it in for that poor apple. So, they gave me a glass of wine as if to say, "Well, it's all over." After all the fucking awful, dirty, shitty things he did to everybody. I said, "Sure, salut," and I threw it on the ground. And he couldn't pick it up. Boy, was he pissed off.

But, you have to separate people from their talent. And, even at the time, I did not want to blow the picture, because it was an important picture. I really felt that it could have been a wonderful movie. But I had to give the very strong impression that I didn't give a fuck and I was willing to blow it all. I just wanted them to get the fuck out of there. I didn't care about going to Africa. And everybody was so overworked and he wouldn't give anybody a vacation.

Wasn't it during the making of this picture that you were thrown off a plane because they thought you were a hijacker?

BRANDO   One time I was coming back from a three-day vacation, dragging my poor ass to the plane in Los Angeles. It was National Airlines, the only connecting flight to Barranquilla for three days. As I got on the plane I said, "Are you sure this is the flight to Havana?" The hostess was tired. She didn't say anything, she just went over and said, "We've got a wisenheimer on here who wants to know if this is the flight to Havana." And the pilot said, "Get him off the flight." [*Laughs*] I couldn't believe my ears. I said, "I'm awfully sorry." She said, "You get off this flight or I'm going to have the FBI man here in a minute." I had a beard so she didn't know who the fuck I was. I got off and ran past the counter and the guy said, "Mr. Brando, wait, what happened? Mr. Brando?" I was running like a sonofabitch, because I knew that he was going to tell the hostess, who would tell the captain, who would call the tower; the tower would call the desk and they were going to stop me and say, "Oh, it's all a big error." I was streaking down that thing like Jesse Owens in the old days. And I looked over to the desk on my way out and the guy said, "Mr. Brando! Mr. Brando, just a minute! That was a misunderstanding. They didn't know . . ." I said, "Listen, if he's gonna be that upset about it, I don't want to be on that flight anyway." Then, of course, it appeared in the papers and all that shit. But I got three extra days out of it that I never would have gotten. Oh, I was never so glad. That was just wonderful.

But then they fooled me, they hired a plane to fly me from New Orleans to Barranquilla.

Did you go?

BRANDO Yeah. I stalled for three days. I guess I had two days out of the three.

Was that the most frustrating of all your films?

BRANDO I never had any trouble like that. Never. It was the first and last. . . .

What about Mutiny on the Bounty?

BRANDO Oh no, that's just all horseshit. Carol Reed wasn't doing the picture that they wanted, and he was taking much too much time. They also didn't have a script. Charlie Lederer, the writer, was on dope, he was shooting heroin. He would appear all rubber-faced and giddy-fingered. So they fired Carol Reed. And then they were blaming me. I said to Carol, "I've got director approval, they can't fire you, I don't know what the fuck this is about." So Carol Reed and I and [producer Aaron] Rosenberg went to this guy's office and they had it out. And Reed quit. The stockholder's meeting was coming up and the next thing I know it appeared in the paper, some magazine article blaming me for the whole fucking thing. They did that to Elizabeth Taylor on *Cleopatra*.

Was that the magazine you sued for four million dollars?

BRANDO *The Saturday Evening Post.* I just couldn't believe that they would do that. They dumped it all on me—its costs, its delays—and then the publicity mills just kept grinding it out. They were making up all these stories and they paid some fella to do a job on me in *The Saturday Evening Post*. So I hired a publicist for the first and only time in my life and said to him, "Listen, I'm not going to hold still for this, find out what's going on." He was Sam Spiegel's public-relations man, Bill something, who later got hit by a taxi—serves him right.

Died?

BRANDO   Yeah. As it turned out, MGM was paying him off. They were paying him a salary and he was telling the head of the studio everything I told him. He wasn't representing me at all. That that should live to haunt you.

Did you ever follow through with your suit?

BRANDO   Yeah. I can't remember what happened, I think they settled, gave me some money.

Was that the only time you've ever sued a magazine?

BRANDO   Yeah, I wouldn't do it again. It's not worth the effort. Magazines want you to sue them. They'll write anything that's scurrilous, that sells a few hamburgers. What they get out of publicity is far in excess of what they pay in lawyers' fees. So Evel Knievel got a baseball bat and broke that guy's arms and leg. I don't think that's such a bad idea.

Especially since you've broken at least one photographer's jaw yourself, when you punched Ron Galella in the mouth

141

when he was taking pictures while you were having dinner with Dick Cavett in Chinatown. Was that the only time you've lost your temper like that?

BRANDO   Oh, I've punched photographers out. Anytime it has to do with the kids, I just go beserk. I can't stand any kind of invasion like that. I can't go to Italy anymore because I'll be in jail. Last time I was there, a bunch of paparazzi were out there. I was saying good night to some guests. I had my son in my arms and I was outside and they started taking pictures. I put the kid down and ran after this guy. [*Laughs*] I took a terrific fucking swing at this guy. I couldn't see, they had lights on me, hell. I missed him and fell on my ass. Then I ran in and got a bottle of champagne and came running out the front door looking for anybody I could get ahold of. One guy jumped on the hood of a car and then on the sidewalk. I followed him, chased him two fucking blocks. He was more scared than I was mad. I reached out to catch him and he jumped onto this streetcar and took off. I went back, two o'clock in the morning, and there's this tough guy banging on the door. My kids are in there, my wife. So I got a knife and I was just going to have it out with him. Tarita was wrestling and fighting me for the knife. "No, don't go!" Then I got myself together and realized what the fuck am I doing? Go out and stab somebody in Italy and it's goodbye, Rachel.

So I went and called the American Embassy and said, "Let me speak to the Ambassador." They said he's asleep. I said, "I don't care what the fuck he's doing, I didn't ask you that, I told you get him on the phone!" I was just pissing mad. Poor guy was intimidated. He got the Ambassador out of bed. "Mr. Ambassador," I said, "I'm being intimidated here and I'm not going to stand for much more of this. You're going to have to make for some arrangements." I went on and on.

The next morning two *carabinieri* are out in front of my house in their fucking uniforms. And a photographer was out there, too. I had to go to work and the guy pointed his camera at me and the *carabiniere* put his hand right over the lens. He had no business doing that at all, it's completely against the law. But they did that, pushed the guy into a car, took him down to headquarters, said, "What have you got here, dope in this camera? Heroin? What is this stuff?" Opened the camera. "Oh, film. Sorry." They never bothered me after that.

In France one time, this photographer was taking a picture of me and my kid. I grabbed him by the tie. I just go fucking beserk. I don't do that anymore, I've calmed down a lot. But I wanted to kill this guy. I don't know why, but the invasion of privacy . . . people don't have any right to do that.

And with Ron Galella?

BRANDO   With Ron Galella, I really had to sit down and talk about that. I broke the guy's jaw. Sure, it was annoying, but then if it's so annoying to me I should be in the lumber business. But the guy *wanted* to get hit. He was looking for some kind of incident like that. People very often instinctively know where to go to get what they want. This guy was following me all day long. Taking pictures while I was on [Dick Cavett's] show. And afterwards Dick and I went to Chinatown to get something to eat and the fucking guy comes around to take pictures. Finally, I started to get exasperated. I went over to the guy and said, "Would you please just take a few more pictures, you've had enough for today, give us a break." He was getting crowds around us. So he said, "Well, if you'll give me some decent poses, take off your glasses, maybe I'll think about it." I didn't think. Just the attitude was overbearing. And that was it. He sued me. Cost me forty thousand dollars. No, it cost me twenty thousand dollars, the rest was taken off in taxes. The last time I saw him he was wearing a football helmet with a feather coming out the top.

Are you a target for lawsuits?

BRANDO   Oh yeah. What they do is, if I sue you for causing me mental anguish because you made some faces at me at a Halloween party—the charge is ridiculous, but I get you in for a deposition, keep after you, have my lawyers do it. When the fee gets to a certain amount, there's nothing you can do, unless you're mad. So you've got to pay off. I've got a guy suing me right now. It's a harassment suit, but he knows I'm not going to quit, so he's going to quit. It's a matter of lawyer's fees. When you know it's going to cost you more to continue it than it is to settle, then they'll keep after you. That's why Howard Hughes became a recluse. He didn't want to show up in court. He used to forfeit. People used to sue him all the time because he wouldn't show up in court. He just paid the money. People made a lot of money off him that way.

Didn't you once sue some cattle firms over some cattle, because you wanted feeders and got breeders?

BRANDO   Some guy took me for one hundred thousand dollars. That was one of those suits. It would have cost me more to get him in a lawsuit than it was just to walk away. I learned a good lesson. I almost never go anyplace, unless to see friends. I hardly ever go anywhere.

You're known to keep friends since childhood. Do any of them talk about you?

BRANDO   None of my friends, if they're my friends, talk. If they aren't my friends they might say something.

What happens to friends who write books about you?

BRANDO   They're not friends to begin with. Friends don't write books. Acquaintances do.

Have you ever read any of those books?

BRANDO   No. Life is not about that. Surely, life is about something other than sitting and reading books about yourself.
   One guy I befriended, Bob Thomas, a good, responsible reporter who wouldn't ever print something you didn't want to talk about, I had a social, friendly relationship with him. And he sat down and wrote a book. It floored me.

He never told you he was writing it about you?

BRANDO   No. All that time he was researching and writing. Really a sneak punch. It's very easy to do that to people, come up on their blind side. Easiest thing in the world to do.

But you can only do it once, and what you lose isn't worth what you gain. I don't know what he gained out of it.

With all your knowledge of and experiences with Indians, have you ever considered writing a book yourself?

BRANDO   Yeah, I have. I got a lot of notes, I don't know why I don't do it. But I've been doing these films.

How do you write?

BRANDO   Talk into a microphone and then have it typed up double-spaced. I once thought of being a writer. I've written many things but I haven't shown them to anyone. I've done a lot of screenplay rewriting, but I've never taken any credit for it.

What do you think of the writing of Tennessee Williams?

BRANDO   His plays are beautiful and effective and poetic. He's an enormously sensitive and cruelly honest person. If there was a man that had a clean soul, he's one of them. He's an important man. A very brave man.

You traveled to see him in Connecticut to audition for Street-car, *didn't you?*

BRANDO   Yeah.

And you ended up fixing his light switches?

BRANDO It was the john that was broken. Here's some more gossip—said it was the light switch and it was the john. [*Laughing*]

Are there many people in your profession that you have a lot of respect for?

BRANDO There are not many people in *anybody's* life that they have a lot of respect for. No. How many people in your life do you have a lot of respect for?

A handful.

BRANDO A handful? Well, same here.

What about Jane Fonda, Robert Redford?

BRANDO I think Jane Fonda has done something. I could see her doing most anything. Redford's certainly been effective in pursuing his interests. Who always sings "I Left My Heart in San Francisco"?

Tony Bennett.

BRANDO Yeah, Tony Bennett. He's been extremely helpful all the way along.

His wife calls him Tony Benefit.

BRANDO [*Laughs*] That's funny. He's a very decent guy, a very kind man.

You've met a lot of people in the world, have you met many extraordinary people?

BRANDO I've never met a movie actor yet that made me fall to my knees in awe and wonder.

Excluding movie actors. Extraordinary people.

BRANDO Yeah, I have.

Who?

BRANDO Krishnamurti. He was an extraordinary man. People are very often extraordinary because of the position they're in. Nehru was a man of great interest to meet. Anybody who is the head of five hundred million people is a man one must be interested in. Not curious about, but interested in. I met the King of Thailand. I met Dan Tinawaga, a Hopi Indian holy man, along with Thomas Pinyaka, also a Hopi Indian and an important spiritual leader. I remember bringing them on the Steve Allen show, long, long time ago. Dan, who's dead now, was about eighty-eight when he was on the show. He could remember being forced into a sheep-dip with poles. They took all the Indians and lined them up and ran them through a sheep-dip, pushing them under so they'd be covered with insecticide. They felt that their bodies should be cleansed according to what they thought cleanliness. He was a man who lived in and witnessed very tragic, horrifying times.

Any others?

BRANDO   Through a friend I met a professional criminal, who had murdered people, spent a lot of time in jail. I was fascinated with his mind. Kind of important, too. And Stella Adler and Kazan were extremely important to me. I don't think I would have been able to ply my trade as well had I not been with them.

What distinguished Stella Adler from other acting teachers? What was she able to show you?

BRANDO   She was a very kind woman full of insights and she guided and helped me in my early days. I was certainly confused and restless. Outside of her phenomenal talent to communicate ideas, to bring forth hidden sensitivity in people, she was very helpful in a troubled time in my life. She is a teacher not only of acting, but of life itself. She teaches people about themselves. I wouldn't want to say that it's psychotherapy, but it has very clear psychotherapeutic results. People learn about the mechanism of feeling. Whether they ever go on to being actors or not, it's irrelevant, they've learned a lot from her.

Stella Adler once said, though, that she never taught you anything, she just opened doors for you and you kicked them down.

BRANDO   I would like to ask you, Vas ya dere, Charley? [*Laughs*] That's the great phrase that sustains me from one problem to another. It's so simple: finally it comes down to saying, Vas ya dere, Charley?

149

One man whom you were impressed with was Supreme Court Justice William O. Douglas. Didn't you once go to see him about something?

BRANDO Yes, I did. I was absolutely tongue-tied. I didn't know what in the world to say. I met him twice. Once in his chamber, he was gracious enough to admit me. I had a briefcase full of notes and wanted to talk about the American Indian. I couldn't put a sentence together. He sat there, "Yes?" He listened attentively. I suppose that intimidated me more than anything, that he was listening. I stuttered around, stammered. He said, "I have to go to the bench now." I said, "Oh, yes, yes, of course, quite so. Goodbye Mr. Justice, Mr. Dougal, uh . . ."

Was that the first time that's ever happened to you?

BRANDO Yeah.

That doesn't seem to happen to people like Bob Hope, John Wayne, or Sammy Davis, Jr., when they meet with politicians like Nixon and Ford. How effective are such people in influencing others to support someone like Nixon?

BRANDO Well, we ate the pudding, so . . . I think it's just window dressing. Politicians go and get a few movie stars to put behind their ears like a political flower. It's parsley. They're just attention-getting devices, like those flags in the used-car lots that wave in the wind, multicolored iridescent things, drive along and they attract your attention for two seconds and that's the end of the show.

But when celebrities lend their names to a thousand dollars-a-plate dinners, it does seem to bring in the money.

BRANDO   They're shills. Political shills.

Do you think that was Carter's intention when he named Paul Newman to be a delegate to the UN concerning disarmament?

BRANDO   [*Laughs*]

Why are you laughing?

BRANDO   [*Laughing*] I wasn't laughing, I was coughing. Something in my drink.

Would you get involved if the President asked you?

BRANDO   I would not be involved in any formal or informal way with the government. If I can be helpful it will not be because I'm an officeholder. I think Paul would be very effectful as a politician. He's an intelligent, personable, fair-minded guy.

That's what some people said about Nixon. Did you find Nixon amusing when he was in office?

BRANDO   No. He was interesting, but in a way any person who was psychologically or emotionally disturbed is. He is a very disturbed man. He was a bright man, but he was bananas at the end. I would have loved to have been a fly on the wall when Nixon and Kissinger got down on their knees to pray.

[*Starts reciting a Hebrew prayer*]. Nixon had a guilt complex—there was something we never found out, something yet untapped. But he structured his fall, like a Tinkertoy pyramid. He was tottering from the top, so he could fall from a high place. He was self-destructive.

What was staggering was not so much what he did but the fact that he was voted into office. Before he was elected there was a poster that went around that had a picture of Nixon saying, "Would you buy a used car from this man?" Most people buy the image, the front, and that's what people did with Nixon.

Would you ever read his memoirs?

BRANDO   No. I think there've been responsible people who've been up that alley and they said there's not much new, it's just some coughing and shuffling, clearing of the throat, and "I didn't do it." Or, "It was all for the good," or "I was misunderstood." And then his prose can't be that overwhelming to want to read it for the sheer poetry.

As actors, how would you analyze some of the key Watergate figures, like Attorney General John Mitchell?

BRANDO   I feel sorry for him. I saw a picture in the papers of Mitchell on crutches coming out of jail. Here was a man brought down to this, and now physically unable to support himself. He was a proud man, Mitchell. He never admitted doing wrong. You could see the look in his face—it was bad enough he was brought down, trying to maintain his dignity, but having made to be immobile and on crutches—that was the lowest, to be physically brought down as well.

Chief of Staff Haldeman and domestic affairs adviser Ehrlichman?

BRANDO Boy, those two guys really fell. They got power too fast. With such power that you can have a war going in Southeast Asia with a phone call, or launch missiles, it can get to you. Especially if you never had it before, power's intoxicating. What got me is that Ehrlichman could never admit it, not even to his family. I saw a picture of him walking as if nothing had happened, and behind him were his children, who were hanging their heads in shame. That was tragic.

When John Ehrlichman went before Judge Sirica during that period, I got a call from his lawyer saying Ehrlichman wanted introductions to some Indians, he wanted to do the Lord's work for some Indians so he could go up before Sirica with his hair combed and his shoes shined saying, "I have been doing the Lord's work, so take that into consideration when you sentence me." We met, Ehrlichman and his lawyer, for twelve hours off and on. I said I would do what I could if he could supply me with some information about Wounded Knee and who the players were. He wrote down three pages about Wounded Knee. Then I went to John Dean, talked to him. He said that Nixon was well informed about Wounded Knee and it was on his briefings of the day, he wanted to know what the developments were. But I can't really go into those details. Ehrlichman hasn't come clean yet. What I want to know is what Nixon had to say about it.

Do you read newspapers and magazines to get your information?

BRANDO   I read *Scientific American, Science Digest, The New York Review of Books, CoEvolution Quarterly.*

Serious stuff. Do you ever lighten it with something like the Reader's Digest, *to keep in touch with the common man?*

BRANDO   *The Reader's Digest* is the most popular publication in America, outside of the Bible, as far as I know. It is the worst piece of trash I've ever seen in my life, it is without reward. I shouldn't say that—maybe they'll do an article about Indians. [*Laughs*] But I think they know it is not the *New York Times Book Review* section, it's not *Esquire,* it's not *Playboy,* it's not *Scientific American;* nor is it a compendium of all that stuff.

What about books? Since I've been here you've been reading Hannah Arendt on totalitarianism, Colby's CIA memoir, Paul Ehrlich on survival. Is that how you spend much of your time when you're down here?

BRANDO   I used to read an awful lot. Then I found that I had a lot of information and very little knowledge. I couldn't learn from reading. I was doing something else by reading, just filling up this hopper full of information, but it was undigested information. I used to think the more intelligence you had the more knowledge you had, but it's not true. Look at Bill Buckley, he uses his intelligence to further his own prejudices.

Philosophers have gone mad trying to find the objective truth. Kant's *Critique of Pure Reason* is a book at least five inches thick. The man went insane trying to find out what was purely reasonable. I've tried to struggle my way into it, but I didn't even get in up to my ankles before I was just undone by it. I started to read it when I was twenty. I gave up, it made no sense at all to me. It's laughable to me now that anybody would try to do that. Yet men keep doing it, trying to find what are the laws that govern our activities? What are the rules, if any, that determine our behavior? Nobody's come up with the answer yet.

Why one reads is very important. If you don't have a good reason, if it's just for escape, that's all right, it's like taking junk, it's meaningless. It's kind of an insult to yourself. Like modern conversation—it's used to keep people away from one another, because people don't feel assaulted by conversation so much as silence. People have to make conversation in order to fill up this void. Void is terrifying to most people. We can't have a direct confrontation with somebody in silence—because what you're really having is a full and more meaningful confrontation.

It's a good thing you didn't express that in the beginning of this interview or it would have been a very short interview indeed. Before we began taping you told me of a recurrent nightmare you have about being sick, in the Korean War.

BRANDO I didn't say the Korean War. It was just being . . . bm it's not a nightmare . . . it just would be horrible . . . to be someplace in a war where you're freezing and sick, you have diarrhea, no way of getting back . . . it would be awful.

I always wondered why people went off to war, get themselves blown apart. The Korean War, the Vietnam War, why would they do it? Why not say, "Christ, I'll go to jail for five years and that will be worth it, but I'm not going to get my head blown off, that's absurd, I'm not going." A lot of them did it. But the number that did not go was not so impressive as the number that went.

When you were of draft age, how did you avoid the Army?

BRANDO   I beat the Army by being declared psychoneurotic. They thought I was crazy. When I filled in their forms, under RACE, I wrote, "Human"; under COLOR, I wrote, "It varies." Also, I got thrown out of military school, which helped.

You must have made your parents proud.

BRANDO   When I was kicked out of military school, my father thought I was a nogoodnik, I wasn't going to amount to anything. When I went into acting, that was the worst thing. To my father, everything was how much is it worth? how much did you get? When I started making money at it, he couldn't believe the kind of money I was making. It kind of blew his mind. He didn't know how to handle it.

How about yourself? How did you respond to the pressure? Did you ever become dependent on drugs or drink?

BRANDO   How individuals or society responds to pressure is the determination of their general state of mental health. There isn't a society in the world that has not invented some artificial means to change their minds, their mood, whether it's cacao or kola nut or alcohol. There are five or ten million alcoholics in the United States. My mother and father were alcoholics. My mother died when she was forty-six or forty-seven. What a way to go. I used to go with them to Alcoholics Anonymous meetings and see some of the most horrid and putrefying sights, alcoholics lying there with maggots eating into their ankles.

But all kinds of drugs have been with man forever and a day. If they're used as a means of escaping from problems, then the problems are only going to increase. Confrontation of problems is the only manner of solution of problems. Problems don't go away. Drugs are not a solution, they're a temporary relief.

A lot of people who can afford it go into analysis to get help with their problems, but those who can't often resort to drugs or alcohol.

BRANDO It would be nice to say that poor people aren't happy, but rich people are snorting cocaine, that's the rich people's drug. When *all* the kids are smoking, dropping acid, taking cocaine, then you have to say there must be something wrong. In the main cities, when you can't walk out in the streets without getting mugged or be in fear of your life, something's wrong. All the rich people do is move further and further away from the areas of trouble.

Until you finally come to an island?

BRANDO Until you finally come to an island.

157

Do you think the rich take cocaine as a means of escape or for pleasure, to enhance sexual activity, as a stimulation, whatever?

BRANDO   If it's a pleasure not to be yourself, not to have doubts about yourself, or to have an exaggerated sense of your own importance, then perhaps it is a pleasure. But it's a questionable one because you're dealing with an unreal world and eventually you're going to have a rendezvous with a brick wall, and you'll have to return to whatever you are.

Well, we all know who you are, at least as an actor and activist, but who would you have liked to have been if you could choose any period in history to have lived?

BRANDO   I think I would have liked to have been a caveman, a neolithic person. It would have been nice to see what the common denominator of human existence was before it started to be fiddled with.

You would have wanted to be, though, a strong caveman?

BRANDO   I would have been Ralph Kramden. Just your average cave dweller.

Then you would have missed the Marlon Brando Film Festival that the L.A. County Museum sponsored.

BRANDO   Oh gee, I missed that. Shucks.

There aren't many film festivals of contemporary actors in museums. It's kind of nice.

BRANDO Kind of nice, I guess that covers it. Better than a poke in the eye with a stick.

Do you often have to upset yourself when acting?

BRANDO How come you want to know about acting all the time?

These are my last shots.

BRANDO What else?

How much truth was there in the reported rivalries between you and Montgomery Clift, or you and James Dean?

BRANDO I think that's beneath me. It's too silly.

I had to ask.

BRANDO I know you had to ask me, but then I had to say it's too silly when you did ask me.

Another such rivalry, according to the press, is between you and Frank Sinatra, stemming from the fact that you got the better role—and better songs—in Guys and Dolls. *Sinatra has apparently called you the most overrated actor in the world.*

BRANDO I don't think that's true. You didn't hear him say that. Vas ya dere, Charley? And you weren't. So, unless he says that to my face, it's not going to have any great significance.

And even if he did say it, I don't know if it's going to break my stride.

The press does play up rivalries, obviously.

BRANDO Of course they do. That's how they make their bread and butter. What else are they going to do, write serious stories about people?

Is it true that you vetoed Burt Reynolds for James Caan's part in The Godfather?

BRANDO Francis would never hire Burt Reynolds.

But do you have that kind of control over who acts with you?

BRANDO Well, you have to have rapport.

Didn't the Italian-American Civil Rights Organization say that you defamed their community with your role as Don Corleone in The Godfather?

BRANDO I don't know. If they said that about me then they must have felt that was true.

Have you had that said about you when you've played different nationalities in your films?

BRANDO No. I played an Irishman who was a freak psychopath [*The Nightcomers*] and I didn't get any letters from any

Irish-American organizations. It would have been difficult to make *The Godfather* with an eighth-Chinese, quarter-Russian, quarter-Irish, and an eighth-Hispanic. Very difficult to take those people to Sicily and call him O'Hoolahan. It seems idiotic, if that's a fact, because most of the people who played small parts in the movie were in the Mafia, and so were their families. So, it must have been a different Mafia these Italian people were talking about.

Did you receive one hundred thousand dollars from Paramount to talk to the press after making The Godfather?

BRANDO I can't remember. When I hear something like that I always remind myself of the Congressman with his hand in the till. Normally I don't do interviews because I want to avoid having people ask me questions that I think are unimportant.

Which is probably what you're going to say with this next question. Does being labeled a Method Actor mean anything to you?

BRANDO No.

Does it bother you?

BRANDO B-O-R-E. Bore.

Is that what a method actor does—to bore through to the core of a character's being?

161

BRANDO It bores through and goes beyond the frontiers of endurable anguish of interviews.

Well, this painful interview is almost over.

BRANDO Oh, listen, it hasn't been painful at all. It's been delightful. Although I feel like I got in a rummage sale: would you want this dress? No, that *schmatte*. How about this corset? Well, we could take the rubber out and make a slingshot out of it. I'm dizzy. We've gone from the temples of Karnak to the halls of William O. Douglas.

Speaking of temples, do you believe in God?

BRANDO I believe there must be some order in the universe. So far as there is order there is some force in the universe. It's hard for me to conceive it's just happenstance or a confluence of disorder that makes the universe what it is.

And are you optimistic or pessimistic about the future of life on this planet?

BRANDO You can't live a life saying, Well, this is the end, so we might as well get out the banjo and the rowboat and get it on, just go laughing and scratching along until Gabriel blows his horn. Whatever the circumstances are, one has to keep trying to find solutions. Even if it seems impossible. They have never invented a system that worked: religion didn't do it, philosophy didn't do it, ethics didn't do it, economic systems won't do it. None of the systems that deal with man's problems have ever worked. But to live a life of hopelessness, it's not possible.

I've heard pros and cons. I've heard scientists say we don't know enough, that the cycle of life on earth is so delicately balanced that if we haven't already thrown it out of kilter then we certainly will by our natures, which seems unstoppable, immutable. Others say there's a great day coming. Buckminster Fuller is a man of hope, positively believes in nirvana of the near future. Herman Kahn has told us what a wonderful world we'll have and the nature of the struggles to get there. Who knows?

You mean you don't have the solution?

BRANDO I don't have a solution to death.

What about getting older? How have you been aging?

BRANDO Rather well. I've gotten happier as I've gotten older. More content.

Are you afraid of death? Do you think about it?

BRANDO "Of all the wonders that I yet have heard, it seems to me most strange that men should fear; Seeing that death, a necessary end, will come when it will come." Another wonderful speech on death.

Do you remember more of Shakespeare than any other author?

BRANDO He's worth remembering. "For God's sake, let us sit upon the ground/And tell sad stories of the death of kings." I can't remember it all. [*Thinks*] "That rounds the mortal temples of a king/Keeps Death his court, and there the antic sits,/Scoffing his state, and grinning at his pomp . . . And with a little pin/Bores through his castle wall, and farewell king!"

It was announced in the papers that you had consented to play King Lear *on Broadway and that Elia Kazan would direct. Yes or no?*

BRANDO No.

Have you willed any of your land to the Indians after you die?

BRANDO No. I have not.

But you have already given some land to them?

BRANDO I gave forty acres to an organization called Survival of the American Indian. I don't know what the status of that is now.

Here's an offbeat question for you: what are things which repulse you?

BRANDO The most repulsive thing that you could *ever* imagine is the inside of a camel's mouth. It's so awful! That, and watching a girl eat small octopus or squid. I mean, I'm not squeamish about anything, I could make an ocarina out of a petrified turd with no problem, but that. . . . There's a certain frog that carries its eggs on its back and after they are fertilized these froglings burst forth from the skin . . . it just makes me sick. I don't like to look at somebody's sticky saliva. These people who laugh—HA, HA, HA—and there's a stringer of saliva from their upper tooth to the bottom lip and it bends every time they go HA HA, it pulsates. Jesus, with one girl you could take her saliva and walk across the street with it and lay it down on the sidewalk and still be connected. The viscosity of some people's saliva is remarkable.

What about something like bullfighting, does that offend you?

BRANDO   I'd like to be the bull but have my brain. First, I'd get the picador. Then I'd chase the matador. No, I'd walk at him until he's shitting in his pants. Then I'd get a horn right up his ass and parade him around the ring. The Spaniards don't think anything more of picking an animal to pieces than the Tahitians do cutting up a fish.

Which brings us, full circle, back to Tahiti. Didn't you once get poisoned from eating a fish here?

BRANDO   It was from the ocean. We all got poisoned. They don't know how it works. You can't eat fish or drink alcohol for six weeks or it will come back on you. Your mouth tingles, you can die, the bottoms of your feet itch, you become mad with itching all over. You get a terrific headache, cannot sleep.

And all this time I've been enjoying the fish we've been eating for dinner.

BRANDO They've got something down here you ought to try. It's called *fafaru*. They take a fish and let it rot in sea water: bacteria, sea water and the fish produce rot. Then they throw out the fish and the water but the bacteria remains. They get more sea water and let this bacteria brew develop. Then they get a fresh fish and put it in this brew to marinate for an hour or six, take it out and eat it. It's just as though they were eating putrid meat. It smells like carrion. What a vulture's head would smell like.

I'll pass on that one.

BRANDO Oh, you've got to try it. Tahitians go after it, gnawing on it like an oxbone. A lot of Tahitians can't eat it. If they do they always sit at one end of the table. I was in Japan once and the *pièce de résistance* at this restaurant was its fresh sea food. They brought out on a plate a live lobster that had been deshelled and it was lying, quivering and moving on this plate. That almost made me get religion.

Let's finish up with some of the experiments you plan on conducting here. A number of the projects you started have been aborted, like the lobster research program and some of your solar energy projects. What else did you have going here?

BRANDO We saved the turtles. Less than a fraction of one percent of all turtles that are hatched live to maturity and return to breed. In the summer months we take the turtles and we hatch them—we bury them so they hatch near us and then we take the little ones and put them in a pen and feed them until they're about a foot across and then let them go. But we almost never get to that point because people steal them before that.

But I thought this was a private island. Who steals them?

BRANDO The people who come over in boats, who come into the lagoon to fish. The lagoon is public. They steal coconut crabs, but they're full of radioactivity. And they swipe pigs. They also come on the land and steal things, burn things, wreck the trees. So many do that we've had the gendarmes coming out here by plane. When I came here the islands were so full of fish you could close your eyes and throw a spear near the coral and you'd stand a pretty good chance of hitting a fish. The lagoons have been cleaned out of fish now, the population of fish has diminished from what it was. Some of the fishermen eat the birds. If the government can't stop them, I can't do it.

But they're your islands.

BRANDO But in the middle of the night, when they come, you can't be up patrolling.

Nonetheless, let's not leave the impression it's Terry and the Pirates *here. It is possible for small groups to visit this atoll for the day or overnight and it certainly is a tranquil and beautiful place to be.*

BRANDO   Yeah. I could open this up for tourism and make a million dollars, but why spoil it?

Do you find it irresistible to leave this place once you're here?

BRANDO   It's very hard. But . . . "miles to go before I sleep, and miles to go before I sleep."

Didn't Marilyn Monroe write that?

BRANDO   I think Marilyn did, yeah. It was either her or Fatty Arbuckle, I can't remember.

AFTERWORD

8 / "I'd Lost Touch with Reality"

The interview with Brando appeared in the January 1979, twenty-fifth anniversary issue of *Playboy*. It was billed as "a candid—if reluctant—conversation with the country's greatest actor." It received a lot of publicity and mail, but the letter I found the most interesting was the one from Marlon dated January 18. It was three pages long, typed, and began: "Disappointment is waned and smoldering resentment is lapsed." With such a beginning I dreaded reading on, but after complaining in the first paragraph that some facts which he considered "vital in respect to Indian matters were arbitrarily, and I assume, casually excised from my conversation," he changed his tone in the next paragraph. "I might add," he wrote, "that you did indeed make me sound more intelligent than I expected from the way I remembered speaking to you. Thank you for that."

He wrote of his "obsessive personality," which made him regret the loss of all he had to say about the Indians and asked if I would send him the complete transcript of our talks so he could use the things he said for some future article. He thanked me again for helping him appear "more organized and articulate" than he felt he was and added that he had been receiving letters praising the interview. "As I put it all together now," he wrote, "our experience seemed to have been a very useful one." Then he tacked on a postscript: "Fuck the press. Unless you know them, and trust them and know them not to be at the mercy of the editors. It's the same old story."

I wrote Brando back and during the next three years I would occasionally speak with him over the phone. Our last, and by far most interesting, conversation was on January 7, 1982. When I wished him a happy new year he said he thought that was a silly thing. "We should celebrate something like the spring equinox, that makes more sense." He knew that my wife was Japanese and asked if we brought in the year changing clothes and cleaning the house and listening to the gong of large bells, which he said he had heard and really loved when he was in Kyoto. "I wonder if they ever made a recording of those gongs. They're so beautiful."

When he asked me what I'd been doing I told him I was interviewing Luciano Pavarotti, following him from New York to Chicago to San Francisco. "Oh, what a wonderful man he is," Brando said, "he's spectacular, extraordinary. I don't know anything about him but I think he is a very primitive man and not too sophisticated or philosophical. He exudes that lovely quality that everybody feels." When I said that Pavarotti finished his first movie (*Yes, Giorgio*) he wondered if it would be very popular "with the punk rock crowd? They're the ones who go to movies.

I guess some still go to see Woody Allen but it won't be Burt Reynolds flying out some window. I can't imagine it would make any money." I told him that Pavarotti was going to do an hour television special before the Academy Awards show. "Maybe he can urinate on the microphones" at the Oscars, Marlon said.

He asked me about my daughter and then talked of an idiot savant he had read about who could give the day any date could fall on within a thousand years. "What useless knowledge," I said. But Brando believed it all fell into some strange scheme of things. He spoke of two sisters in England who spoke simultaneously and how tests were run to see if one talked before the other and apparently they didn't.

When I asked him about his kids he said that Cheyenne was dancing, playing the piano, painting, and socializing a lot. "I want to bring her here as little as possible." Teihotu was in college in Hawaii and loved it there. "He's six feet tall and such a gentle and beautiful boy, like a Greek statue." Christian, Brando's oldest son, was staying with Marlon and had a girlfriend. Teihotu was also visiting.

When I wondered what ever happened with his lawsuit against the Salkinds, the producers of *Superman,* he said, "That's all settled. I got fourteen million dollars. They had to defer it until this year. After taxes it's about seven or eight million."

"Not bad for a couple of weeks' work," I said.

"Wasn't a couple of weeks, it was twelve days," he laughed. "It's so ridiculous. Absurd." He went on about the Industry, how they were all "liars, it makes me so sick, it's amazing, the people in the movie industry. Even Francis

Coppola owed me one-and-a-half million and I have to sue him. They all do that, because they make interest on the money, fifteen or twenty percent interest, so they delay paying and then you pay lawyers and it's all lawyers. The Salkind brothers tried to buy me out after the picture was made for six million. And those pricks at Warner Bros. It's so ugly, Larry. I hate the idea of having to act, but there's no other way to do it."

When I brought up *The Formula* he said he thought it was "a terrible piece of shit. They cut that all to pieces. They took out all my humor. But I didn't have any money and I did it for the bucks. Ten days for three million bucks. I didn't care."

There was a buzzing of Brando's intercom as Teihotu wanted to tell him that he was going with Christian to get a haircut. Marlon wanted to know if they were taking his car and they negotiated for how long. "Two hours? Three hours?" Marlon asked. "Hard to say," his son answered. "Well, let's say you'll be back in four hours then." Teihotu said he'd try, but reminded Marlon that he'd be with Christian. "Okay, don't let Christian drive like a nut," Marlon said. "Do you need any money?"

When he got back on the phone I asked him when was he last in Tahiti. He said a year ago. The house he was building when I was there is still being done. But he built a school and wanted to activate it, devoted to the Tahitian culture, the sea, and modern technology, to show the people that they don't have to depend on the West, they have their own culture and it's far better than ours. "They're happy people, they have that to offer. They think they are of no consequence but they have a vast contribution to make to the world. While the world is fighting and killing each other, stabbing and strangling, they're there responding and laughing and having children. It's a joy."

Then Marlon segued into terrorism. "Can you imagine what it's like being a friend of Carlos, the terrorist? Thinking, 'Well, maybe we should blow up Bullock's, or get through the air conditioning system, or I know a gas line that leads to. . . .' I try to imagine what they're like when they're not being terrorists, when they're fucking, eating, picking pimples, getting wax out of their ears, watching the leaves fall. They can't be terrorists all the time. But that's their work, that's what they do."

Terrorism led to the Palestinian struggle in Israel. "I think Israel is going mad," he said. "They're living with a siege mentality. If the UN adopted a resolution for a military presence in the Golan Heights and all the countries agreed to it, it might be a solution of sorts." The Palestinians, he was convinced, ran the Middle East. He wondered how that area could have such conflicts when all the religions came from there and there were similarities in the languages and the music.

"I've never been to Israel," he said, "but I'd like to go." He spoke of once visiting Egypt on his way to India and being impressed with the Sphinx. And he was reminded of an Israeli he met who was working on turning sewage into food for pigs by running it through algae. The man sent him some of these pellets to eat, which Marlon did, and he got indigestion.

"Maybe he meant for you to feed them to your pigs and not take them yourself," I said.

"I think we're going to live to one hundred twenty-five,"

175

Brando said, changing the subject to organ transplants. Then he mentioned a psychiatrist who came up with Logo therapy. He had survived the concentration camps because he had a meaning. He studied the camps and what went on and saw that life became meaningless for others, but as long as you have a sense of meaning you can go on. He was struck by Will Durant dying a few weeks after his wife Ariel did. Gave up his will, his meaning. "Did we ever talk about Hannah Arendt?" he asked. "About the will to follow? Put on a uniform and run up Hamburger Hill. I can never understand that."

I brought up what happened to Patty Hearst and mentioned that when I had interviewed her in San Mateo I had the feeling that our conversation was being bugged. "Oh sure," Marlon said, "as we speak there could be sophisticated listening devices like a laser beam aimed at a window which could pick up everything. Voices can be magnified and filtered. They can do it with anything, any electrical impulse can be translated; sound, light, and vibrations are all interchangeable. It's shaky times. The reported crime rate is up, Justice Rehnquist is hooked on pills, he's a drug addict, Mrs. Ford is on drugs, the whole country is on drugs. Everyone has to chemically barricade themselves against the effect of cultural tensions. We're absolutely coming apart, and it's going to get worse as the economy does. The white collar workers are being laid off, and now the blue collar workers who voted for Ronnie Reagan are getting it in the ass. I think the controls are with the CIA and the FBI. I've talked with Russell Means and the Indians and they're always monitored. It's so easy to bug anybody, who's going to know? You can unscrew your phone and take out the mouthpiece and put one in with transmitters and it can transmit whatever you're saying."

When he began to talk about the new science and the double helix I mentioned a script I had completed, a genetic engineering thriller.

"Oh my God, right up my alley," he said and began talking about how we'll be crossing a chicken with an elephant, and how it's a revolution that's occurring. "Wheat will grow in the winter like crocus. It will alter our world in the next twenty-five years, the graph is vertical. The change, the society of the future, is all happening now. Who the fuck knows what they're doing? There's more experimentation now than Hitler ever dreamed of, being done on terminal patients . . . put a chopped-up Ping-Pong ball in someone's nose.

"If you could make that feasible," he went on, "that's the trick. You know, with the CIA experimenting on people using LSD. I thought Legionnaire's Disease was a CIA experiment that got out of hand. Bacteria on people. . . ."

His interest made me realize that Brando could still be stimulated by a good story. He even began to plot locations (I had set it in Washington) and talked about distribution and direction. "You can make a lot of money in movies if you don't spend anything," he said. "If you make them outside the country, with talented people, not with big name actors, and avoiding the unions. You make it up as you go along. Give the cinematographer nothing, give him one-half percent of the picture. Use natural actors. Do it at a cost of two million dollars. Jesus, you do a film here, it's endless. A cheap film is six million dollars. The unions kill you. You could direct it yourself. Anybody can direct. You could even act. Everybody wants to be in the movies. It's very simple. Don't do it with a studio. The main thing is to make it credible so people can believe in the fantasy. The CIA has been used to death with Redford and others. Make it reasonable. No actors. Find a colorful background like Macao or Tangier, some place that's got smack to it. Washington is dull, just a bunch of buildings. Haiti is a good place to do it. With the moonlight, the rain. Drums in the background. There's a huge set there that's never been used, the Citadel. Get the Haitians to work for a dollar-fifty a day wages. Kickback some money to the Tonton Macoutes. Of course, there are a lot of black people and people don't like that. Have a Bahamian corporation, you'd be able to make some big bucks. Shoot it in sixteen millimeter. Get a release to distribute it, that's a little difficult. But you have a nose for facts and for research. I don't know how you write drama but most of it is improvised anyway. *Last Tango* was the best opportunity for improvising. I wrote a lot of that movie. As dialog. And you make that part of the improvisation. De Niro and Scorsese are able to do that kind of stuff. Another good way to write it is to get actors together. Let them talk. Or bring in the people you are portraying and ask them to talk, that way you get the real thing. But hell, I don't even know your story and I'm telling you all this."

I asked him if he was involved in any stories himself and he said "I wrote a film. It's six volumes, very rough and unfinished, way overwritten. It's an interesting story—actually I wanted to do it about Tahiti to get money to run the school there."

When I asked him what his story was about he told me

in his rambling, discursive manner. "It's about a smuggler in Hong Kong who gets out of jail. He had saved a Chinese guy's life while in jail who happened to be one of the . . . well, there was this pirate named Lee Choy San in 1927 and . . . well, I got so involved in the research that I forgot about the project.

"There was this pirate, Madame Chang, who in 1830 controlled six hundred junks and I don't know how many people, pirates, and she fought the Chinese navy to a standstill. There were many women pirates, and many supported Mao Tse-tung, but that's jumping ahead. Anyway, these pirates were raping China and cutting China up around 1911. And this guy, this smuggler, steals from the pirates these pearls from the Royal Palace worth half-a-million dollars. Only these pirates have a network of information.

"The smuggler goes to Tahiti, where he has a wife and children, and then he wants to go to Valparaiso and on to Paris. He's a kind of romantic figure who has pretentions of being a writer and writing the great American novel, but he's this smuggler, and he meets this very beautiful girl who gets stuck—this is all taking place on my island.

"The owner of the island is a French dilettante painter who's very social and knows all the politicians. He has a polo field on the island. And this beautiful girl is having trouble with her passport and is forced to have sex with the French guy. There are these shots at imperialism and the colonial mentality.

"Well, the girl turns out to be a huge crook. The guy has smuggled these pearls and gives one to her. How he does it is he gives her a drink, a Singapore Sling, and when she gets to the bottom she gets the pearl in her mouth worth around fifty thousand dollars. She says, 'How did this get here?' and he acts like he doesn't know. But his wife is on the island and he feels guilty about this and doesn't know what to do."

Struggling to make sense of this story so far, I thought back to when Marlon told me that guilt was a useless emotion. I didn't dare interrupt as Brando continued with his meandering tale.

"Then there's this other woman, a tourist who writes for something like the *American Way* and she's doing these interviews for pieces on the South Seas and she's getting the guy's story—a real pain in the ass, but she's really a detective hired by Lee Choy San to find him (his name is Dultry)."

At this point Brando interrupted himself and chuckled. "Aren't you glad you asked me about this?" I didn't respond, but he was in the mood to talk and the story continued.

"Well, the guy ends up kicking the shit out of a bad guy, breaks his legs, leaves him tied up under a coconut tree, and leaves. A coconut falls from the tree and kills the bad guy. Dultry makes his way to a boat and as he goes there a police station blows up in front of him. Out in the water there's this dark black junk and Lee Choy San, who is a patriot, has come to get the pearls which were taken from the Royal Household.

"It ends with him escaping. He sinks the junk. He and the girl are going to get on a boat. She goes to get her hair fixed—he hasn't fucked her because she's too beautiful and he wants it to be just right—and the boat takes off. He goes to the bar and then he can't find her. But he gets this note from her saying: 'Sorry Dultry, but you're not in my plans.' She took all of the pearls and is on a tramp steamer going in the other direction. He sees her and gets off the boat and goes after her.

"Back on Tetiaroa he sees the mess and chaos and death there. And this piano—he loves the piano—is on the beach and he winds up furiously playing the piano and settling down with his wife. The end."

After hearing this I'm speechless, not knowing if Marlon has made this all up at the spur of the moment or if he really has worked on this story. He didn't ask for my opinion but I ventured to finally say that it sounded like a Clavell-type story, fat and juicy, with women pirates and stolen pearls, Chinese junks, and a piano on the beach. But what I was really thinking about were those T. S. Eliot mermaids. Perhaps, after all, Brando has heard their song. And he's out there on the beach with his piano accompanying them.

"Marlon," I said, "why don't you write a book?"

"I think it's okay to make a living out of writing," he said, "if you know very clearly what you're doing. But there's something so pompous about writing to me, so presumptuous, as if you're the bearer of the Holy Grail, like you have the magical elixir and if people would only listen to your wisdom everything would be all right. Actually what it is is just people shooting their mouths off."

"So, your memoirs are not in the future?"

"Books are too formalized," he answered. "I don't know what to write about. I've started to draw lately. I started out drawing things and plants but I couldn't draw plants, so I started drawing faces."

"Are you any good?"

"I don't think so. I draw faces of people and I put remarks

they might say above them. I'm fascinated . . . I could look at my bathroom floor for *hours* and see faces there or on the wall or in the trees. Since I've been drawing I see things differently. I can look at a coat over a chair and it's quite another thing."

"What do the people who work for you think about your staring at the bathroom floor for hours?"

"I got rid of everybody in my house," Marlon said. "I did my own cooking, my own cleaning. I was losing touch with being alive. I'd press a button and say, 'These grapes aren't big enough, I like them the size of my fist and these are only as big as my thumb.' I wasn't doing anything, just sitting like a beached whale. I'd lost touch with reality."

Six years later Ava Gardner told me this story about the time Brando invited her to see a documentary about the Indians. "We went in and saw this stuff about the famine and the misery and poverty of the Indians," she said. "Then we went back to his hotel near Central Park. The place was crawling with Indians all in saris. They were all India Indians. We sat on the floor and had a drink. I wasn't wearing a bra and all of a sudden Marlon reached over and grabbed me in the breast, completely impersonal like a doctor, and said, 'Are those real?' I said, 'I believe they are.' He intended to shock me . . . and he did."

9 / "My Son Is No Mad-Dog Killer"

A far more serious and shocking reality would force the reclusive Brando reluctantly into the spotlight when, on May 16, 1990, a death occurred in the living room of his house on Mulholland Drive. Earlier that evening, his first son, Christian, thirty-two, and his twenty-year-old Tahitian daughter, Cheyenne, had gone out for dinner. Cheyenne was pregnant by a Tahitian man named Dag Drollet, who had come to see her. But Cheyenne was unhappy with Dag. According to Drollet's father, Dag couldn't deal with Cheyenne's erratic behavior and had flown to Los Angeles to break off their relationship. But Cheyenne told her half-brother Christian a different story over dinner. Drollet, she said, beat her. They had bad arguments. She was very upset. She dreamed of seeing him crucified. Christian, who had a problem with alcohol, continued to drink as they talked, telling her, "I'm going to bust him!" By the time they returned to their father's house he was pretty stewed. He saw Drollet sitting on the couch watching TV, got his gun, walked up to Drollet and fired a round into the Tahitian's left cheek, killing him instantly.

Because of Christian's last name, the shot was heard around the world. Marlon was in another part of the house with Tarita when the shot was fired, and when they entered the living room and saw what had happened Tarita bent down to touch Drollet as Marlon wept. He instructed his son to call the police and wait for them to arrive. If Christian had any intention of fleeing the scene, Marlon made sure he would face the consequences of his actions like a man.

When the police arrived, Marlon explained what had happened and Christian was booked on murder charges. Marlon called William Kunstler, an old lawyer friend from his civil rights days, and Kunstler flew to Los Angeles to help build Christian's defense. "I didn't want to shoot him," a distraught Christian told the police. "If I did, I wouldn't do it in my father's house. We were both in a fit of rage and the fucking gun went off. It's my fault because I had a loaded gun in the house. I had a few drinks in me. We struggled and blewey—he's dead."

Like a modern Greek tragedy, the deeds of the son came to haunt the father. Marlon Brando could no longer avoid the media, which began to stake out his house and the courthouse where Christian would be arraigned. Marlon appeared at the courthouse with members of his family and sat quietly behind Christian as charges were made. "The messenger of misery has come to my house," Marlon told the media. "To those people who have known these kinds of tragic circumstances in the world, no explanation is necessary. To those people who do not know the nature of this acute misery that both our families suffer, no explanation is possible. We must just be strong and I think that the family, with love and [by] supporting each other, will prevail."

At first, no bail was set, because there was a concern that Christian might leave the country. Then bail was set at ten million dollars and Christian's passport was to be surrendered to the court. The bail seemed outrageously high and Marlon realized that he would have to face the press and show himself to be what he was: a worried and concerned father who wanted his son to receive a fair trial. The media—reporters, photographers, television crews— was thick outside the courthouse when Brando appeared before them.

"If I were a poor man under the same circumstances as a tree surgeon or a dental assistant, there wouldn't be all these cameras here," Brando said. "I wouldn't see myself on television, none of that would happen. But I have to fight hard to preserve that sense of reality in order to bring up my children in a very real life. I have nine children with four different women and I have bonded with those children at a very early age and when you become a father you become a father for life, that's simply the way I feel about it. [This incident] hasn't brought our family any closer, because we are as close as we can be."

He spoke of how he had not brought up any of his children to expect privileges and benefits because their father was a famous man. "Christian is a welder," he said, "Miko works for Michael Jackson, my daughter Rebecca worked as a waitress, my other daughter . . . Petra, has worked for a law office and wants to be a lawyer. Teihotu is working as a fisherman and is also captain of a ship on the island.

So they've all put in time, they're not sitting around waiting for the good goods. I've had them open the door and look for the Porsche on their birthdays and I've said, 'No Porsche out there.' I don't even know how to spell it. It's tough . . . to go through the experience of being famous. There is a downside to it, it robs you of your reality."

To emphasize the point he reminded the media of his own reclusive behavior. "You all know me, I don't rush out to this restaurant, to that restaurant, to see if I can get my picture taken. I've been tough to get at. Because I really wanted to preserve a sense of reality about my life in the glare of what has come to be known as celebration. I want to turn my back on that and I find that it's difficult. When somebody assaults me—I don't personally care what anybody says, you've never seen a suit that I have ever made against anybody for anything that was ever said about me—but when it comes to my children, that's quite a different matter."

He rambled on about his son's good qualities, vowing that they would fight to keep Christian from being convicted as a first-degree murderer. The killing, the Brandos believed, was an accident. A crime of passion, not one of cold-blooded intent. "My son is no mad-dog killer," Marlon said. "There is another Christian and I hope to have the opportunity to present it in court. Christian has been depressed. He should not be punished simply because he has a father who happens to be well-known."

When asked what advice he had given to Christian, Brando replied, "I don't think I've said anything that would not be said by any father. I just kept telling him, 'Sometimes in life, you have to duke it out.' That's what he's going to have to do. But he's tough, and I'm proud of him."

Defending his son's plea of not guilty, Brando said, "I know in my heart . . . Christian never lied to me once. He knows he's an alcoholic and on occasion has taken drugs, and thereby broken the law. But he's never lied to me."

Looking back on his own youth, Marlon tried to distinguish who he was from the public personality he had become. "I went to the ranch when I was fourteen, I milked cows, I cleaned stalls, I shoveled horse manure, I dug ditches, I did a lot of very hard work, so I remember what it's like to earn two bucks. I'm remembered that way in my mind, I'm that person, my name is Buddy Brando. Then suddenly I became Marlon Brando. My father turned to me once and said, 'Marlon, what do you think . . .' and I said, 'What are you talking about?' He had called me Bud all my life."

Admitting to being uncomfortable in the spotlight, Brando apologized for "blathering on" and told the press, "I don't respond properly or conventionally to questions. I don't read stories about me and I don't even see my own movies. This is a false world. It's been a struggle to try to preserve my sanity and sense of reality taken away by success. I have to fight hard to preserve that sense of reality so as to bring up my children."

He brought up the problem of alcoholism in his family, a problem which he once talked to Truman Capote about more than thirty years ago, then regretted ever since. It wasn't a subject he liked to talk about, yet here he was, telling the world, because it might help people understand and be more sympathetic to his son.

"I've had maybe five alcoholics in my family and maybe the genetic feature of that alcoholism was passed on to Christian," Marlon said. "Every time you get knocked down, when you stand up, you're smarter. Christian has had a problem of alcoholism from the time he was fourteen. I won't go into the story of his mother, you know it all too well, it's been through the courts forever and a day, and I don't need to answer for her, she speaks for herself. I was in court about fifteen times on visitation rights and custody— I fought like hell, because I knew what was happening to him and by the time he was fourteen the judge let him make up his own mind who he wanted to be with, and he didn't choose his mother, he chose me. By that time he'd been through some pretty hefty times."

Stories began to appear in newspapers and magazines about Christian's lifestyle and the arsenal of guns he had collected, including a MAC 10 machine pistol and an M-14 assault rifle. The young man had worked as a tree-surgeon and a welder, had appeared in an Italian gangster movie, had had a number of girlfriends, and generally had had a confusing, directionless life.

Cheyenne, it would come out, was in bad psychological shape. She suffered from depression, contemplated suicide, and had had a disfiguring car accident in Tahiti the previous year. "She has suffered a head injury," Brando would tell the press, "in which . . . she had to have her face remade." Cheyenne would claim that Marlon was not her father; that he used to lock her in closets, which wasn't true; that he was jealous of her life and happiness; that he was fixated on his movie role as the Godfather and expected her to take care of him. It was revealed that she took drugs that may have affected her mind, and soon after the shooting she returned to Tahiti to have her baby. She wanted no part of Christian's trial.

"Cheyenne is visiting with a psychiatrist," Marlon told the press, "she is under control of the courts, she had to surrender her passport, and she is having a great struggle within herself to regain her emotional equilibrium. It is not, as some of you might think, because of the events that took place in my house. She was troubled. And there is another story to that, which I will spare Mr. Drollet and which I will spare you for the moment, that has to do with some rather unsavory, unattractive, and unfortunate occurrences that came to pass before this event at my house took place."

At a later press conference, Brando was more forthcoming. "Cheyenne has suffered enormously," he said. "She's been beaten physically. We have clear proof of that." He said that she had suffered "a nervous breakdown," and had to excuse himself for crying when telling that his daughter was "doing her best" and that the child she had given birth to, a boy named Tookie, was "fine, healthy, strong."

For Brando to talk so openly about family matters, for him to reveal that there were "unsavory" occurrences that had nothing to do with the shooting of Dag Drollet, and for him to shed tears in anguish showed just how far he was willing to do what was always so odious for him: to lay out his dirty laundry for the public to see. It went against everything he believed, this intrusion of his and his family's privacy, but he was fighting for a larger cause, he was fighting for his first son's life.

"When it comes to a District Attorney assaulting my children and my family and saying and implying things and feeding private information that was contained only in the police records to the media, what chance have I got?" he asked. "What would you do as a father in my place? Would you not be obliged to stand up, and since you are thrust in this public position, respond to it? I can do no other."

The District Attorney, who had fought against Christian's bail at any amount, and who was convinced that he would leave the country if he received bail, was clearly the target of Marlon's animosity. After Christian was arrested, pictures soon appeared in the press that made him look like a thug, with his eyes drooping and his face unshaven.

"The most egregious thing that [the D.A.] has done is to employ the carrion-oriented press to make sensational stories out of this," Marlon said. "Everybody has gone for a day-and-a-half unshaved. When that picture was taken of Christian, he had not shaved for a day, and he was tired, he'd been kept up all night, he'd been grilled by the police, and bang! there was that face. Then they had another pose of him taken by somebody who had him looking back, like the Hillside Strangler. My son isn't a mad-dog killer and I hate to see him, I hate to see *anybody*, portrayed that way. We all know, and [the D.A.] knows very well, what the value of a picture is, what the value of a pose is, what the value of an expression is. If I were to have a picture taken while I was saying 'Well . . . ,' I'd look like a nut. And that's what a lot of you wait for," he said to the photographers who elbowed each other to get their pictures. "Which is perfectly all right because you're in the news business, you're selling something, and that's something that sells a lot more."

When he was asked if he thought the shooting incident could have been avoided, Brando demonstrated his unconventional response to such a question. "Where is a feather dropped by a sea gull on the heads of two thousand persons going to land?" he asked. "There are so many unknowns."

When a reporter asked him, "What's the best you can hope for when your son does come to trial?" Marlon responded: "I would think the best that I could hope for would be accidental manslaughter. That is what I believe, that is what our experts, who are famous around the country, who have worked both sides of the street, the defense and the prosecution, that is the conclusion that they have come to, that it is accidental manslaughter."

Soon after it was announced that Brando had set up a $1 million trust fund for Dag Drollet's four-year-old daughter from a previous relationship, Christian's bail was reduced to $2 million. Brando put up his house, and after nearly three months in jail Christian was released pending his trial. On that day Marlon was at the jailhouse to get him. "He got thinner and I got fatter," Marlon said. "I'm very happy to have him back, we're going to go home now and do whatever Christian wants to do."

Still irked by the attitude of the D.A., Brando added, "When I went to court today I looked him straight in the face and I asked him if this course of events, the judge giving Christian the opportunity to be free during the interim, has changed his conception that Christian is the blathering mad-dog killer that he has portrayed him to be in the press. And he said, 'No.' I don't know what he'll have to say when we do come back."

Brando's return to the front pages of the news and entertainment sections of the press did not just rest on his son's pulling the trigger on his daughter's boyfriend. Two months after that incident his first starring film in over a decade appeared. It was a comedy called *The Freshman,* and Brando brought back his godfatherly role as Don Corleone, only this time, sending up his famous character.

Marlon's involvement with the film came about after writer/director Andrew Bergman found out that Brando had admired his 1979 black comedy, *The In-Laws.* Bergman sent Brando a script of *The Freshman* and received an invitation to discuss it with the actor in Tahiti. Once there, Bergman and producer Mike Lobell were treated to Marlon's "anxiety test," as they waited nearly a week before *The Freshman* was brought up. But eventually, after acquiescing to Brando's suggestions (and his $3.3 million fee plus 11 percent of the gross), they returned with that rarest of industry coups: Brando's agreement to be in their movie.

The movie was shot in Toronto, Canada, in 1989 and costarred Matthew Broderick, who told reporters how his knees quaked when he first met the legendary star. "We were waiting for Marlon to come," Broderick said, "and I was so hysterically nervous. I kept turning the stereo on and off and adjusting the speakers. I'm not normally like that, it was all Brando-related. And then he came in wearing a sweatsuit and sunglasses and he gave everybody a big hug. But when we sat down to read the script, I was too scared to even open my mouth. It was terrifying."

But once the young actor settled down, he found Brando to be a father figure. "I don't know how to explain it," he said, "but when you act with him all his attention is on you. There's nothing self-conscious. You feel like you're being taken care of—like you're in very good hands."

Director Bergman said he had no idea how "playful Marlon was," and thought he was "like a bad boy—on the set, he's not an intimidator, he's a practical joker." Bergman, along with everyone else, was impressed with how riveting Brando could be with even the slightest of props, like crushing a walnut in his hand. "Brando physicalizes things so brilliantly," Bergman said. "That's always been his great secret—how he uses the smallest props and how he acts with his hands. There's such a simplicity about him. You can't take your eyes off him." Brando's huge bulk contributed to his overwhelming presence, but as Brando's other directors knew and Bergman discovered, "You're never conscious of him acting. He likes to keep it fresh. That's why he never does a line exactly the same way twice."

By the end of August it became apparent that the film would not be completed on schedule and that Tri-Star Pictures would have to pay Brando $50,000 for an extra day's work. But when that money was not forthcoming, Brando called a reporter from *The Globe and Mail* and wound up giving a widely quoted interview where he disparaged the production. "This picture, except for the Canadian crew, was an extremely unpleasant experience," he said. "I wish I hadn't finished with a stinker. It's going to be a flop, but after this, I'm retiring. I'm so fed up."

Marlon went on to call the film his "swan song" and took yet another shot at the movie business, saying, "I suppose I'm unjustified in railing against it, but when they start talking about art, they hospitalize large numbers of people from laughter."

After Brando's remarks were published, Tri-Star came through with their payments and Marlon retracted his statements. "I have of late been experiencing some very trying times of a personal nature," he explained. "I have seen enough of [*The Freshman*] to be able to say with confidence that it will be a very successful film."

Although it wasn't a big commercial success, the reviews of *The Freshman* were solidly favorable. Brando's role was singled out and most reviewers agreed with Los Angeles *Times* film critic Peter Rainer, who wrote of Brando's "minor miracle. By all rights, watching America's finest actor parody one of his greatest roles should be a sorry spectacle—a sign of artistic bankruptcy. Brando acts so infrequently that, when he does, you want him to do something great, something *fresh*.

"Except that he does indeed do something fresh. The role is nothing more than an elaborate comic turn, but he invests it with such sly knowingness and reserves of feeling that he gives this dinky joke-book movie a soul. Brando is doing here what a lot of famous actors probably wish they could do to the roles that made them famous (or, in Brando's case, famous again). He's using the gravity of his performance in *The Godfather* for comic effect, bringing out the absurdity that was always just under the surface of the role.

"For years, Brando's Godfather was perhaps the most heavily parodied of all contemporary performances. (The take-offs were a back-handed tribute.) Why shouldn't Brando join in the fun? What *The Freshman* demonstrates is that Brando can parody himself better than any of his imitators—and still appear as regal as ever."

Said Chicago *Sun-Times* critic Roger Ebert, "Other actors satirize themselves, and we are embarrassed for them. Old movie tough guys like George Raft used to turn up on TV, ripping off their own famous lines, and it was humiliating. But when Brando plays Don Corleone in *The Freshman* . . . it is not an embarrassment, it is a triumph, because Brando is still *playing* him, still acting, every moment, in character."

As Ebert watched the movie he found himself "amazed by how overwhelming Brando's performance was," and came to reflect upon the actor's authority: "By one means or another, Marlon Brando has learned, over the years, to dominate a scene more completely than any other living actor. He is not performing, he is there. He is a fact. And behind the fact are the shadows of our memories of all his other performances."

The previous year, Brando had appeared as a liberal lawyer fighting apartheid in South Africa in *A Dry White Season*, another mesmerizing performance that earned him an Oscar nomination for Best Supporting Actor. And, in spite of his saying that *The Freshman* was his swan song, he seriously considered acting in David Lean's *Nostromo* until the trouble with his son made his family a more pressing priority.

In late September 1990, Brando also managed to shake up the publishing world by contradicting his belief that celebrity books are presumptuous and announcing plans to write his biography, "to set the record straight." Offers in the millions began pouring in, as publishers began jockeying for position to publish whatever kind of record Brando wanted to leave. "The fact that he would be willing to do a book is itself interesting enough for a publisher to want to pursue it," said the president of Simon & Schuster's Pocket Books. Editors who knew Brando's address wrote to him directly, saying what an honor and privilege it would be to be his publisher. Others contacted his lawyer in London, wanting to be sure they had a chance at what was being considered the jackpot of all celebrity memoirs.

But bids on his book, as well as any future movie projects, were put on hold when, on November 1, five days before Christian's trial was to begin in Los Angeles, Cheyenne took an overdose of tranquilizers and antidepressant drugs and was rushed to a Tahitian hospital in a coma. Dag Drollet's father, Jacques, believed it was a suicide attempt brought on by "the nearness of the trial . . . and too many family difficulties." Because Cheyenne was considered the prosecution's key witness after having told the police that her halfbrother intentionally shot her former lover, Christian's trial was once again indefinitely postponed. Brando again blamed the Los Angeles District Attorney's office for his daughter's problems. "This case is tearing everyone apart," he said. "I hold them directly, not indirectly, responsible for her present mental and physical state." He then questioned Cheyenne's value as a credible witness. "She has given six contradictory versions of what happened on the night of the sixteenth of May to five different people. To any jury she would hardly be a believable witness."

Brando prepared to fly to Tahiti the following day to be with his daughter, but was advised against it by his lawyers because French authorities there would not guarantee that he would be free to leave in time to attend and be a witness at his son's trial. The examining Tahitian magistrate hearing the case involving Dag Drollet's death (Cheyenne was charged in a complaint filed by Jacques Drollet) told a news conference, "If Mr. Brando came to Tahiti to see his daughter, he would very certainly be heard as a witness." Under French law, only that magistrate could approve Brando's return to the United States. "It's beyond wrenching," Christian's defense attorney said of Marlon's dilemma. "It's an impossible decision for a father to have to make." Christian, who returned to welding as he awaited his trial, became seriously depressed when Cheyenne entered the hospital and began seeing a psychotherapist.

Then, on November 11, came more unsettling news. Cheyenne, who had come out of her coma and was released from the hospital, put a rope around her neck at four in the morning and attempted to hang herself. She was again rushed to the hospital and placed on a respirator. A distraught Brando told the press that she was expected to live, "but we don't know if there's been brain damage or not." He hoped that the D.A.'s office would finally stop their maddening attempts at bringing Cheyenne back to testify at Christian's trial. "[Are they] going to bring a girl back who one week takes an overdose and one week tries to hang herself?"

He said that Cheyenne was "the most precious thing in the world to me," but cursed the legal system that prevented him from going to Tahiti to be by her side. "The fucking judge is going to arrest me," he said. "They would detain me by taking my passport, and I'm stuck in Tahiti. . . . I could be down there a year."

The "messenger of misery" continued to stalk Brando and his family. For a man who had given so much of himself in his films, who redefined a masculine code on screen, who put so much of his private life and resources into social and political causes in which he believed, and who went as far as he could from the public eye to seek the privacy he preferred, his son's struggle for freedom and his daughter's battle for her life seemed an overwhelming burden.

Nine days later, on November 20, Deputy District Attorney Steven Barshop announced, "If we determine that Cheyenne Brando cannot come to the U.S. because it would be detrimental to her physically or emotionally, then we will not pursue her further."

Cheyenne had been hospitalized five times since returning to Tahiti in June and was currently in a psychiatric ward, but Jacques Drollet still believed that she was being prevented from testifying against Christian by her family. She "knows things and she wants to tell the truth," he said. "She's not crazy, she's very sound and clear. Her family and Marlon Brando are keeping her away."

In December a French court in Tahiti declared Cheyenne mentally incompetent to handle her own affairs or to care for her newborn son, and her mother, Tarita, was appointed as her guardian. On December 21, a Santa Monica Superior Court judge agreed with the French court, ruling Cheyenne to be "mentally disabled." In his five-page decision, Judge Joel Rudof wrote that prosecutors had provided him with "insufficient information to permit this court to further endanger what appears to be a fragile mental condition and attempt to have Miss Brando returned."

Deputy D.A. Barshop publicly expressed his personal disappointment but acknowledged that without Cheyenne he did not have a murder case. "Without her, we cannot legally prove malice, and without being able to prove malice, this case is a provable manslaughter. With her, this case is a murder—at least, a tryable murder."

The county prosecutors agreed to a plea bargain and on January 4, 1991, Christian pleaded guilty to voluntary manslaughter, where he could serve a maximum of sixteen years in state prison. Jacques Drollet was angry and skeptical, saying "Marlon Brando is rich, and well known, and his lawyers are very clever. They will find a way to get Christian out."

But Christian's lawyers weren't *that* clever and in February, just before his sentencing, a Los Angeles County probation report recommended that Christian be sentenced to three years in state prison. The probation officer had concluded that "this unassuming, low-profile, low-self-esteemed person is not viewed as an individual who could premeditate a murder. In essence, it is felt that a series of unfortunate actions led to the victim's death." The report also detailed Christian's traumatic life, beginning with the custody battles between his mother and father, his several kidnappings by one or the other parent, his molestation by one of the hired kidnappers, and the abuse he suffered by his alcoholic, mentally ill mother.

Before shooting Drollet, the probation report concluded: "He remembers how it felt to be helpless and having no one to help when one fears. No doubt the defendant heavily identified with his sister. With the defendant having a fondness and affection for his sister and having past memories of fear and helplessness, it appears that he acted emotionally to his sister's indication of physical abuse."

But the day after this report was released Christian granted an interview to the Los Angeles *Times* where he expressed doubt over whether Cheyenne had ever really been beaten by Drollet. "I feel like a complete chump" for believing her, he said.

He admitted to being nervous and "scared to death" and was willing to serve his time in jail. He spoke of growing up "with an extremely violent mother. She drank and we had a lot of problems." Anna Kashfi's absence from Christian's trial underscored the distance between mother and son, and Christian said that he had not talked to her in three years.

But it wasn't just his mother who presented problems for him. "My family's so weird and spaced out," he said. "We'd have new additions all the time. Like I'd sit down at the table with all these strange people and say, 'Who are you?'" More often than not, these strangers would tell him they were his half-brother or -sister.

Christian's psychiatrist, Dr. Saul Faerstein, also spoke up. Neither Marlon nor Anna Kashfi provided "a stable, protective, safe, emotional environment for Christian to grow up in," he said. "He is a tempestuous kid from a tempestuous family, frustrated and angry about his life."

On the day Christian's sentencing hearing began, his father wore a red band around his ponytail, his half-brother Miko wore his hair long, and Dag Drollet's parents—Jacques and Lisette LeCaill—came to see if their sense of justice would prevail. Testimony was heard that attempted to show that Christian had a history of violent conduct, including a charge of former wife abuse, but that testimony was refuted the following day when Christian's ex-wife swore he never beat her. On the third and last day of the hearing Santa Monica Superior Court Judge Robert Thomas listened patiently as a tearful Marlon Brando took the stand to speak on his son's behalf.

After refusing to take the oath—"I will not swear on God," he pronounced—Marlon agreed to speak the truth under penalty of perjury. He said that the only reason he married Christian's mother was because she had gotten pregnant. Then he owned up to being less than a responsible husband and father. "I led a wasted life," he said. "I chased a lot of women and she was very jealous." Though he found Kashfi "probably the most beautiful woman I've ever known . . . she came close to being as negative a person as I have met in this life, as cruel."

Brando noted that Anna Kashfi never attended her son's hearing, which demonstrated the kind of mother she was. He said that Christian had gone through so many upheavals as a child that by the time he was a teenager he was "a basket case of emotional disorders."

Digressing, distressed, Brando attempted to shoulder some of the blame for his son's action. "Perhaps I failed as a father," he said. "The tendency is always to blame the other person. There were things I could have done differently. . . . I did the best I could."

When Christian's lawyer asked him about the public's perception that his son was a spoiled child of a rich and famous man, Brando got angry. "Either they're a lying son of a bitch or they don't know what they are talking about," he answered defiantly. "Of all my children, Christian is the child who from the very beginning has been the most independent. I've offered money to Christian and he wouldn't take it. . . . He wanted his own identity and he worked hard to get it."

He claimed, bitterly, that had his son been poor, black, or Mexican he wouldn't be going through this ordeal. Then he dramatically looked towards the throng of photographers and reporters and stated, "This is the *MARLON* Brando case."

Brando spoke for nearly an hour, finally turning to Jacques Drollet and his wife and apologized, in French, to them. "I cannot continue with the hate in your eyes," he said. "I'm sorry with my whole heart."

Christian, too, stood and apologized to the Drollet family. "I'm sorry," he said. "If I could trade places with Dag, I would. I'm prepared for the consequences."

Judge Thomas then pronounced a ten-year sentence for Christian—seven years more than the family anticipated, six years less than the prosecutors wanted, and far less than Dag Drollet's family felt he deserved. "He's getting away with murder, definitely," Jacques Drollet told the press.

"The only thing everyone can agree on is that this was a tragic situation for everyone it touched," said Judge Thomas.

There was nothing more to say.

With his son's fate finally decided, and with his daughter under psychiatric care in Paris, Marlon Brando could finally feel some sense of relief. The children would survive. They had all been through an emotional wringer. Now Marlon contemplated whether or not he'd like to review his life by writing the book so many publishers had expressed an interest in. One deal he was considering involved three projects: his autobiography; another book about the Indians in which he would pen the introduction; and a movie—a remake of Tennessee Williams' *Cat on a Hot Tin Roof*, with Madonna as Maggie and Marlon as Big Daddy. The deal he finally made was just for his own story.

But if this project goes the way of *The First American* television series and his Chinese/Tahitian/pirate script, both of which have yet to be realized, there will certainly be others to fill his remaining years. He may have preferred to have been a caveman and to have lived in neolithic times, but there is no escaping the fact that should he so desire Marlon Brando could continue to define the era in which he now lives.

Postscript

When this book was conceived, the trouble in Marlon's family hadn't yet occurred. The intention was more towards a celebration of the man, as well as a glimpse at a side of Brando other books haven't covered. I was lucky to have had the opportunity to spend some time with Brando— both at his island in Tahiti and at my home in Los Angeles. I found him to be an unusually stimulating and interested man; he could amuse, he liked to be amused, he was always *thinking*, and his powers of observation were acute. I liked being with him, looked forward to seeing him, and knew that when we were together I would never be bored.

I had hoped that he would like this book—at the least, that it would remind him of a time in his life after many of the battles he had fought with studios as well as over social issues were behind him, and when most of the decade of the Eighties was still before him. But then came this tragedy with his son Christian and his daughter Cheyenne, and suddenly the ending changed. I have tried to report the events as they have unraveled, realizing that modifications occur almost daily and that there will be no ending to all of this. Life will go on, the family will somehow get through their anguish, and Marlon will be a different, and forever changing, man. At the end of Joseph Conrad's *The Heart of Darkness*, which was also used in Francis Coppola's *Apocalypse Now,* the character Brando plays on the screen whispers, "The horror. The horror." Words that seem apt and appropriate to describe the agony of what Brando and his family are having to go through in this last decade of the twentieth century.

Acknowledgment

Since 1977 I have been lucky enough to be associated with what I consider the fairest, most in-depth print interviews in the English language, and probably in the world: those which appear monthly in *Playboy* Magazine. Yet, when I go to libraries to do my research I often find that the *Playboy* Interview is not readily available. Librarians, I guess, associate *Playboy* with pictures rather than words and thus deprive researchers of what is often considered to be the definitive word portrait of a particular subject. This has always puzzled me. I believe that not enough credit has been given to Hugh Hefner and to the *Playboy* editorial staff for having the foresight to include such broad and far-ranging conversations with some of the more interesting people in our popular culture within the pages of their magazine.

All three of my books—*Conversations with Capote, The Hustons,* and this one with Marlon Brando—had their beginnings with *Playboy,* and I am grateful to Mr. Hefner, and to editors Barry Golson and Arthur Kretchmer, for trusting me to get a job done and for allowing me the freedom to do it.

The Films of Marlon Brando

The Men   (1950)

A Streetcar Named Desire   (1951)

Viva Zapata!   (1952)

Julius Caesar   (1953)

The Wild One   (1953)

On the Waterfront   (1954)

Desirée   (1954)

Guys and Dolls   (1955)

Teahouse of the August Moon   (1956)

Sayonara   (1957)

The Young Lions   (1958)

The Fugitive Kind   (1960)

One-Eyed Jacks   (1961)

Mutiny on the Bounty   (1962)

The Ugly American   (1963)

Bedtime Story   (1964)

The Saboteur—Code Name Morituri   (1965)

The Chase   (1966)

The Appaloosa   (1966)

A Countess from Hong Kong   (1967)

Reflections in a Golden Eye   (1967)

Candy   (1968)

The Night of the Following Day   (1969)

Queimada! [Burn!]   (1970)

The Nightcomers   (1972)

The Godfather   (1972)

Last Tango in Paris   (1972)

The Missouri Breaks   (1976)

Superman   (1978)

Apocalypse Now   (1979)

The Formula   (1980)

A Dry White Season   (1989)

The Freshman   (1990)